IMAGES of America
FARALLON ISLANDS
THE DEVIL'S TEETH

On the Cover: Egg-Pickers at North Landing, Southeast Farallon. Chickens hadn't arrived in San Francisco during the Gold Rush, and eggs were a rare and valuable commodity. Wild murre eggs were an acceptable substitute, thus an egg rush began on Southeast Farallon that lasted for more than two decades. It is reported that by 1856 between three and four million eggs had been taken. (Stereographic card by Enno Nesemann; California State Library.)

IMAGES of America
FARALLON ISLANDS
THE DEVIL'S TEETH

Marla Daily
Santa Cruz Island Foundation

Copyright © 2019 by Marla Daily
ISBN 978-1-4671-0397-8

Published by Arcadia Publishing
Charleston, South Carolina

Library of Congress Control Number: 2019935946

For all general information, please contact Arcadia Publishing:
Telephone 843-853-2070
Fax 843-853-0044
E-mail sales@arcadiapublishing.com
For customer service and orders:
Toll-Free 1-888-313-2665

Visit us on the Internet at www.arcadiapublishing.com

AULONE ISLAND, FINGER ROCK, ARCH ROCK (HOLE IN THE WALL), AND SUGARLOAF, FISHERMAN'S BAY, SOUTHEAST FARALLON ISLAND, 2014. This book is dedicated to the members of the All Eight Club, and to the biologists, ornithologists, geologists, anthropologists, and other explorers who have an insatiable curiosity to learn more about California's offshore islands. Visit ISLAPEDIA.com. (US Fish and Wildlife Service.)

Contents

Acknowledgments 6

Introduction 7

1. 19th-Century Sealers, Naturalists, Artists, and Photographers 9
2. Egging and the Southeast Farallon Egg War 25
3. From Keepers of the Light to National Wildlife Refuge 37
4. Into the 21st Century 55
5. Wildlife on and around the Farallones 73
6. Extraordinary Seabirds 89
7. Plants Both Native and Introduced 105
8. The Devil's Teeth Are a Hazard to Navigation 113
9. Shark Park and the 30-Mile Swim 121

Acknowledgments

This book is made possible by the Santa Cruz Island Foundation (SCIF), established by Carey Stanton (1923–1987) in 1985 to protect and preserve the cultural histories of the California Islands. Historic photographers from more than a century past—Carleton Watkins, Eadweard Muybridge, and Oluf Heineman—set the stage for others who followed. Warm thanks are due to those who shared their island images: biologists, botanists and natural historians Gerald Carr, William Everett, Steve Junak, Jean Pawek, Virginia Skilton, and Brent Stewart; photographers of the natural world Alan Grinberg, Tom Haglund, Dan Harding, Richard Jackson, Frans Lanting, James Mosquito, Steve Munch, David Pereksta, Giancarlo Thomae, Jack Swenson, and Steve Young; great white shark men Scot Anderson and Ron Elliott; David McGuire and the extraordinary marathon swimmers Joseph Locke and Kimberly Chambers. In addition, Point Blue personnel have logged half a century's worth of images, many of which were selected to illustrate this story. Thanks to Scarlet Hutchin, Oliver James, Oscar Johnson, Ron LeValley, Dan Maxwell, Ross Nichols, Rory Stansbury, Jim Tietz, and Sophie Webb. Annie Schwartz is singled out for her dedication to recording the natural history of Southeast Farallon. Lishka Arata provided office assistance.

Images were also provided by 25 institutions across six states and Washington, DC: Bancroft Library, UC Berkeley; California Academy of Sciences (CAS); California State Library (CSL); Carnegie Museum of Art; Fine Arts Museums, San Francisco; J. Paul Getty Museum; Jepson Herbaria, UC Berkeley; Mariners' Museum; Museum of Fine Arts, Boston; Museum of Vertebrate Zoology, UC Berkeley (MVZ); National Archives; National Oceanic and Atmospheric Administration (NOAA) with special assistance from Robert Schwemmer; New Britain Museum of American Art; New York Public Library; Prelinger Library, San Francisco; San Francisco Maritime National Historical Park (SFMNHP); San Francisco Public Library (SFPL); Santa Barbara Botanic Garden (SBBG); Santa Cruz Island Foundation (SCIF); Stanford News Service; US Coast and Geodetic Survey (USCGS); US Coast Guard (USCG); US Fish and Wildlife Service (USFWS); US Lighthouse Society (USLHS); and the Beinecke Library, Yale University (BLYU).

Thank you, Bill Dewey, for your professional contemporary HABS photographs. Special thanks are also due Peter White for authoring the 1995 seminal book on the Farallon Islands, and to Gerry McChesney, US Fish and Wildlife Service, for access to the Farallones. Thank you, Millie Sunbear, for your technical assistance, and Jaimie Jenks, for your help.

Most of all, I thank my extraordinary husband, Kirk Connally, for sharing his love of islands with me. Mil gracias to all!

Introduction

There is an intrinsic quality of mystery shared by islands throughout the world. What is on them? What is familiar? What is new and different? These questions naturally come to mind with each new island experience.

The Farallon Islands are a group of small, rugged islands and sea stacks in the Pacific waters off the coast of San Francisco, California. They lie nearly 30 miles due west of the Golden Gate and 20 miles south of Point Reyes, and span a seven-mile stretch from northwest to southeast. On clear days, they are visible from the adjacent mainland. Collectively, the Farallones consist of over 20 small islets divided into four groups: North Farallones, Middle Farallon, South Farallones, and Noonday Rock. A major bank, Fanny Shoal, lies off Noonday Rock. Only Southeast Farallon Island, barely accessible by boat during calm seas, supports historic structures, several of which are maintained for management purposes. It is also the highest Farallon, with Tower Hill reaching 358 feet above sea level. In their entirety, the Farallon Islands lie within the city and county of San Francisco.

The first European to leave record of the Farallones was English privateer Sir Francis Drake. On July 24, 1579, he landed to collect seal meat and bird eggs to take aboard his ship, *Golden Hind*. Drake named them the Islands of St. James, and today one of the rocky islets in the North Farallones still carries the name. Composed 25 years later, the 1603 writings of Friar Antonio de la Ascención, a member of Spanish explorer Sebastián Vizcaíno's expedition, state the following: "Six leagues before reaching Punta de los Reyes (Point Reyes) is a large island, two leagues from land and three leagues northwest of this are . . . seven farallones close together." The word *farallón*, *farallónes* in the plural, is Spanish for "pillar" or "sea cliff." The 1775 writings of Spanish naval officer Juan Francisco de la Bodega y Quadra again refer to Los Farallones, and the name has stood ever since.

In the 19th century, with Mexico's successful revolt against Spain in 1821, the Farallones fell under Mexican ownership. During the first half of this century, the Farallones were exploited by Boston ships and Russian vessels carrying fur hunters and sealers who were drawn to harvest the dense populations of otter, elephant seals, fur seals, and sea lions. From 1819 to 1839, Russians maintained an onshore sealing station on Southeast Farallon Island, and they also harvested seabirds for their feathers and down. Goods were shipped to their headquarters at Fort Ross. French sea captain Auguste Duhaut-Cilly sailed by the southernmost Farallon in 1827 and counted the "crude dwellings of about a hundred Kodiaks stationed there by the Russians of Bodega." The 1848 Treaty of Guadalupe Hidalgo ended the Mexican War, and Mexico ceded California, including the Farallones, to the United States.

In 1848, so too began the California Gold Rush, with news of gold drawing more than 300,000 people to California. Chickens were not yet in San Francisco, and eggs were singular and expensive. In 1848. "Doc" Robinson and his brother-in-law ventured to the Farallones, collected wild murre eggs, sold them in San Francisco, and made $3,000 on their one and only trip. Others soon joined this new "egg rush," and it is said that by 1856 between three and four million eggs had been taken from Southeast Farallon. In 1863, "The Great Egg War" was fought over egg-collecting rights, and two men were killed. With the development of a large chicken industry in Petaluma, California, in 1875, egg collecting activities began to decline, and in 1881 the federal government removed all egging companies, although murre-egg-taking continued on a smaller scale into the 1900s.

As the name *Farallones* suggests, these islands stand as a hazard to navigation. More than two dozen major vessels and countless smaller vessels have gone down at the Farallones. Year-round fog, dangerous winds, currents, and storms often led ships onto the rocks to be pounded to pieces. Until the 1850s, California coastal lighthouses were nonexistent, and charts were incomplete and often misleading. In 1852, Congress created the Lighthouse Board, which in 1853 built a large stone house as keeper's quarters on the flats of Southeast Farallon. Atop the island's highest point, a lighthouse was constructed—the sixth in California. The light, with its first order Henry-Lepaute Fresnel lens, was lit for the first time on January 1, 1856, by lighthouse keeper Nerva Wines. Even with the lighthouse in operation, in 1858, the three-masted ship *Lucas* foundered on the Farallones during dense fog and 23 lives were lost, prompting the call for a fog signal. The first one, installed very cleverly, used a naturally occurring blowhole with a whistle attached, powered by natural wave action. It was destroyed in 1875 by high seas, and in 1880, a coal-fired, steam-operated fog signal was built. Several more replacements followed. Two larger, more comfortable Victorian keepers' quarters, divided as duplexes, were constructed in 1878–1880. But 19th century life on the island remained harsh and isolated, with the lighthouse tender calling only quarterly. Keeper William Beeman lost two sons during his duty, one to drowning and one to fever; and Keeper Cyrus Cain lost three of his children on the island, one to drowning and two to diphtheria.

Activity on the island increased in the 20th century. The Navy built its own weather station on the island in 1905; in 1909, Pres. Theodore Roosevelt created the Farallon Islands National Wildlife Refuge, to protect the breeding grounds of the vast numbers of seabirds and marine mammals. The following year, the Lighthouse Board gave way to the Lighthouse Service (1910–1939) for management. In July 1939, the Lighthouse Service was merged into the Coast Guard. The Navy increased its island presence before and through World War II, building multiple barracks, infrastructure, and buildings while maintaining a radio station and secret transmitter on the island. After the war, the Navy withdrew most of its people, leaving Coast Guard personnel to continue with their lighthouse duties. The Navy closed its radio station in 1965; in 1970, the fog signal was taken out of service; and with automation of the light, the last coast guardsman left the island in 1972. Doors of environmental opportunity were opened.

In 1968, management of the Farallones was assigned to the US Fish and Wildlife Service. Farallon Refuge was expanded in 1969 and 1974, with two-thirds of the island chain designated as wilderness. Biologists from Point Reyes Bird Observatory (PRBO) visited the island in 1967 and were permanent visitors by the end of 1968, monitoring and recording information on a dozen seabird species, migratory birds, five species of seals and sea lions, and white sharks. Their environmental work resulted in a cooperative management agreement with the US Fish and Wildlife Service in 1972. In 1981, Pres. Jimmy Carter created the Gulf of Farallones National Marine Sanctuary, encompassing 1,279 square miles north and west of San Francisco. It was expanded to 3,295 square miles in 1985 and rebranded the Greater Farallones National Marine Sanctuary, managed by the National Oceanic and Atmospheric Administration (NOAA). In 2013, PRBO became Point Blue Conservation Science, celebrating 50 years of Farallones conservation in 2018.

Because of the important and sensitive seabird and mammal populations that use the Farallones as breeding grounds, the islands are not open to the public. The only human inhabitants are a few biologists and refuge staff on Southeast Farallon. Visitors can explore the islands by boat, at speeds of five miles per hour and from a football-field distance most of the year for excellent viewing of globally significant wildlife populations.

One
19TH-CENTURY SEALERS, COLLECTORS, ARTISTS, AND PHOTOGRAPHERS

THE DEVIL'S TEETH—FARALLON ISLANDS, CALIFORNIA. The Farallon Islands lie almost 30 miles outside the entrance to heavily populated San Francisco Bay. Over 20 islands, islets, sea stacks, and rocks are identified geographically within four groups: South Farallones, Middle Farallon, Noonday Rock, and North Farallones. Collectively, 19th-century sailors knew them as "the Devil's Teeth," in reference to their extreme hazard to navigation. Politically, they are within the jurisdiction of the City of San Francisco, County of San Francisco. (Point Blue.)

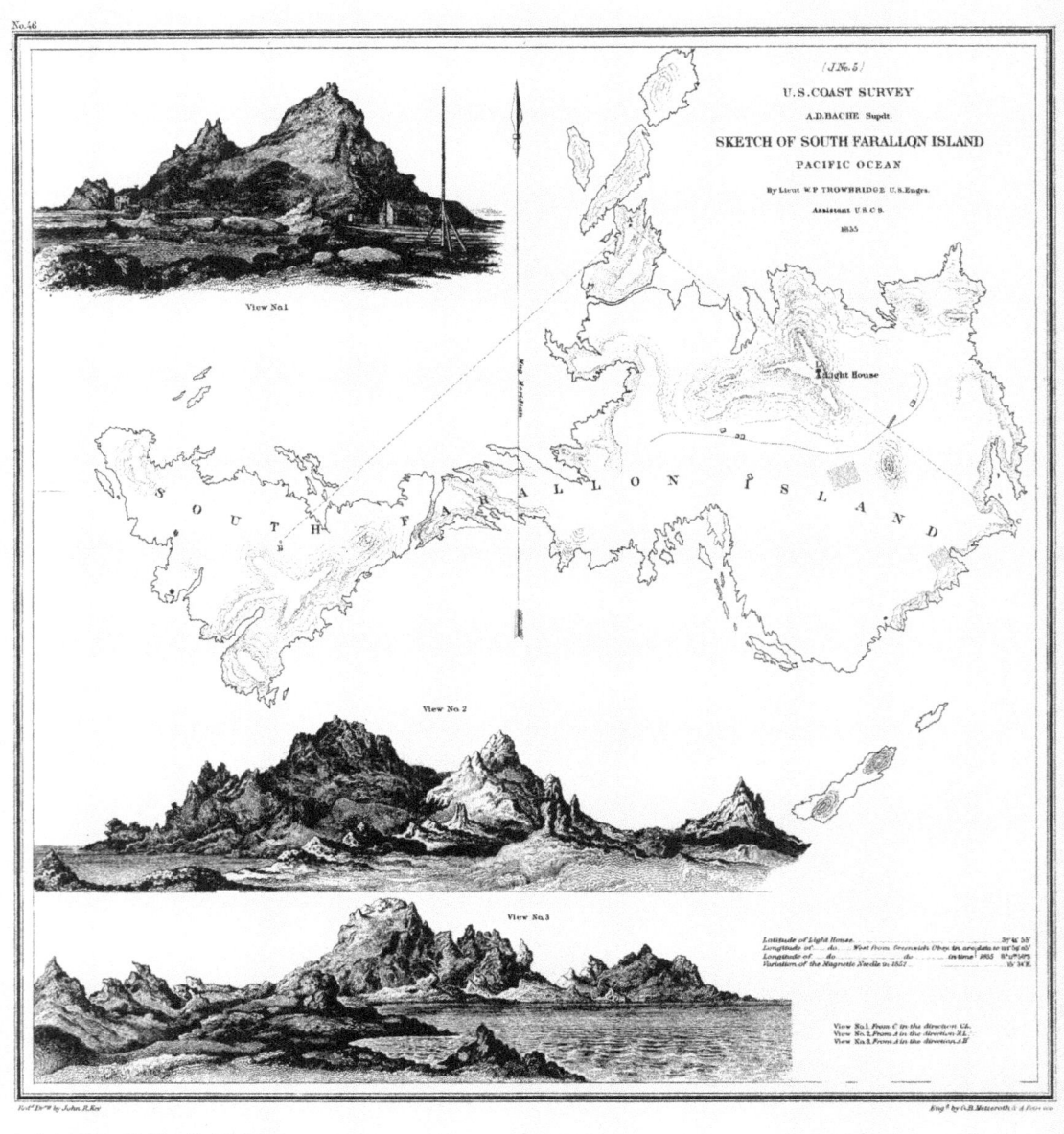

US Coast Survey Map of Southeast Farallon Island, 1855. This earliest coast survey map of the Farallones was done by Lt. William Petit Trowbridge (1828–1892). An Army captain, Trowbridge was placed in charge of the first West Coast tidal observation party for the US Coast Survey from 1851 to 1856. Trowbridge was a civil engineer, scientist, and author who also made extensive natural history collections. He later became a vice president of the American Association for the Advancement of Science and a member of the National Academy of Sciences. (SCIF.)

SOUTHEAST FARALLON ISLAND SKETCH BY WILLIAM P. TROWBRIDGE, 1855. Trowbridge included this detailed sketch of Southeast Farallon Island, which shows several stone houses and smaller structures on the island by 1855. He noted in his report to A.D. Bache, superintendent of the US Coast Survey, "It is difficult to imagine a more desolate and barren place than the South Farallon." (SCIF.)

RUINS OF A RUSSIAN STONE HUT, 1904. Human occupation of Southeast Farallon Island began in the early 1800s with the arrival Russian fur traders. By 1817, they had built a permanent outpost of several stone structures on the island, administered by the Russian colony at Fort Ross. Elephant seals were harvested for their blubber; fur seals, California sea lions, and Steller sea lions were harvested for their pelts. Eggs from common murres were taken by the thousands, and feathers and down were sent to headquarters. Russians left the Farallones by 1840. (Bancroft Library.)

GEORGE DAVIDSON'S SKETCHES OF THE FARALLONES, 1881–1883. George Davidson (1825–1911) was a noted scientist, surveyor, astronomer, and important member of the US Coast Survey for half a century—from 1845 to 1895. Davidson was superintendent of the survey on the West Coast from 1850 to 1857. In the early 1880s, he sketched a number of views approaching the Farallones by vessel. (USCGS.)

SADDLE (SEAL) ROCK AND SOUTHEAST FARALLON ISLAND. Over 20 islands, islets, sea stacks, and rocks, spanning a seven-mile stretch of the Pacific Ocean, are identified geographically within four groups: North Farallon Islands, Middle Farallon Island, South Farallon Islands, and Noonday Rock. Nineteenth-century sailors called them "the Devil's Teeth," in reference to their extreme hazard to navigation. (Photograph by Annie Schmidt; Point Blue.)

NORTH FARALLONES. The Northern Farallones are two clusters of scattered rocks and sea stacks, the tallest of which rises 155 feet above the sea—the island of St. James, named by Sir Francis Drake in 1579. Other islets in the area have Spanish names: Piedra Guadalupe, Peñasco Quebrado, and Farallón Vizcaíno. There are no anchorages or landing places among them. (Photograph by Robert Schwemmer; NOAA.)

NOONDAY ROCK, FARALLON ISLANDS. Five kilometers west-northwest of the North Farallones lies Fanny Shoal, a submerged bank three kilometers in extent. Noonday Rock, a pinnacle wash rock with two 20-foot-high spots separated by a saddle, is the shallowest point of the shoal. This popular dive destination was named for the January 1, 1863, wreck of the Boston clipper ship *Noonday*. (Photograph by Robert Schwemmer. NOAA.)

FISHERMAN'S BAY, SOUTHEAST FARALLON, C. 1878. North Landing, the first landing used on the island, was developed in a finger inlet in Fisherman's Bay on the north side of the island. A derrick was installed to hoist supplies ashore, and a tall wooden ladder gave access to egg-pickers and lighthouse keepers and their families. (Photograph by Carleton Watkins; BLYU.)

STONEHOUSE, SOUTHEAST FARALLON ISLAND, C. 1871. Under the direction of Hartman Bache, a large stone house was built in 1853 as lighthouse keepers' quarters on the flats of the marine terrace below the lighthouse at the base of Tower Hill. The stone was quarried on the island. The house, one-and-a-half stories high, was built to accommodate the lighthouse keeper and three assistants. Upstairs were two 15-by-20-foot bedrooms, each with a fireplace. In the 1870s, an agent of the Pacific Egg Company lived under the same roof. The Stonehouse served keepers until two New England–style duplexes were built in 1878–1880 to accommodate keepers and their families. (Photograph by Eadweard Muybridge; BLYU.)

FINGER ROCK, SOUTHEAST FARALLON ISLAND, 1904. Finger Rock is located at Fisherman's Bay, sandwiched between Aulone Rock and Arch Rock. Norway-born San Francisco photographer Oluf Johan Heineman (1880–1947), who was a member of both the California Camera Club and the Cooper Ornithological Club, visited Southeast Farallon with ornithologist Milton Ray and Charles A. Love in May 1904. (Photograph by O. J. Heineman; Point Blue.)

GREAT ARCH, SOUTHEAST FARALLON ISLAND, 1904. The coastline of Southeast Farallon is dotted with rocky irregularities and indentations, fissures, surge channels, and sea caves. A spectacular large arch on the island's western extremity, 113 feet tall, is dubbed the Great Arch, or Mur Bridge, named for the common murres that sit upon the arch each spring. (Photograph by O.J. Heineman; Point Blue.)

EYE OF THE NEEDLE, C. 1869. Photographer Carleton Watkins (1829–1916) was born in Upstate New York. He ventured west in 1848 to strike it rich, but instead of prospecting for gold, he acquired a talent for photography. Throughout the 1860s–1870s, Watkins masterfully photographed the remote American West. The Farallon Islands were among his favorite subjects. (Photograph by Carleton Watkins; J. Paul Getty Museum.)

SUGARLOAF, C. 1869. Sugar Loaf is about 200 feet high, and according to the *Coast Pilot*, sometimes wave spray goes clean over it. Carleton Watkins captured Sugarloaf arising from a swirling mist of waters at Fisherman's Bay by lengthening the exposure. His technical photographic achievements, particularly under adverse conditions, were unmatched in his day. (Photograph by Carleton Watkins; Metropolitan Museum of Art.)

SHAGS ON THEIR NESTS, FARALLON ISLANDS, C. 1870S. Three species of cormorants are found on the Farallon Islands, where they nest in colonies. They are all fish-eaters, and they dive for their food. Photographer Carleton Watkins was not afraid to venture up cliff faces to capture his images. (Photograph by Carleton Watkins; CSL.)

RUNNING THE ROOKERIES, C. 1870S. In this extraordinary photograph, Carleton Watkins captured at least 13 egg-pickers working the slopes of Southeast Farallon Island in search of murre eggs. Watkins marketed and sold over a hundred different scenes from the Farallones, particularly through the sales of stereographic cards. (Photograph by Carleton Watkins; CSL.)

THE CAVE, WEST END, FARALLONE ISLANDS, PACIFIC OCEAN, C. 1870S. Southeast Farallon Island is pocked with numerous land and wave-carved sea caves, both unnamed and named: Great Murre Cave, Rabbit Cave, Body in the Cave, Jewel Cave, Lost World Cave, Pastel Cave, Sea Garden Cave, Spooky Cave, Corm Blind Cave, Cricket Cave, and others. Rabbit Cave is the largest known cave on the island and is located on the southeast-facing slope of Lighthouse Hill. (Photograph by Carleton Watkins; CSL.)

SEAL POINT, C. 1870S. Farallon Islands' craggy peaks and rocky shorelines, dotted with marine mammals and thousands of seabirds, provided unique and dramatic photographic opportunities for early photographers such as Carleton Watkins, Eadweard Muybridge, O.J. Heineman, and others. (Photograph by Carleton Watkins; CSL.)

TOWER HILL AND PARROT ROCK FROM THE BATH, C. 1869–1871. Eadweard Muybridge began his exhaustive career as a landscape photographer in San Francisco in 1867. His large photographs of Yosemite Valley made him world famous. From 1879 to 1871, Muybridge was commissioned by the government to photograph the lighthouses of the Pacific coast, including the Farallon Island light. The name Parrot Rock came from the fact that puffins were also called "sea parrots." (Photograph by Eadweard Muybridge; CSL.)

BREAKER COVE, SOUTH FARALLON ISLAND, C. 1869–1871. Photographers Eadweard Muybridge and Carleton Watkins were contemporaries living in San Francisco in the 1870s. They both ventured independently to the South Farallon Islands to capture the dramatic scenery, taking multitudes of photographs, which were sold in the form of stereoviews, two almost identical photographs side by side on curved cardboard and viewed through a stereoscope, producing a three-dimensional effect. (Photograph by Eadweard Muybridge; CSL.)

FARALLON ISLANDS, CALIFORNIA BY ALBERT BIERSTADT, 1872. Artist Albert Bierstadt (1830–1902) was a German-born American painter best known for his lavish, sweeping landscape paintings of scenes in the American West. Bierstadt traveled to Southeast Farallon Island on April 29, 1872, aboard the 130-foot revenue cutter *Wayanda* with Professor Wilkinson. They stayed on the island until May 1, 1872, departing on the same vessel. (Fine Arts Museums, San Francisco.)

SEAL ROCK BY ALBERT BIERSTADT, 1872. Albert Bierstadt likely became familiar with the Farallon Islands through the contemporary stereographic views by photographers Carleton Watkins and Eadweard Muybridge. The islands' strange rock formations and isolated windswept terrain, teeming with sea lions and seabirds, would have been a natural attractant to a landscape artist. (New Britain Museum of Art.)

SEALS ON THE ROCKS BY ALBERT BIERSTADT 1887. Bierstadt painted at least 16 large oil paintings from his earlier 1872 Farallon Islands sketches. Many repeat the same combination of dramatic seas and waves, rocks and arches, and bobbing sea lions, often with one grasping a pink fish in its mouth as seen here in the water in the center foreground. (Carnegie Museum of Art.)

SEAL ROCKS, FARALLONES BY ALBERT BIERSTADT, 1872. Albert Bierstadt's arrival on Southeast Farallon Island at the beginning of 1872 coincided with the sea lion breeding season. He spent three days executing numerous on-the-spot oil sketches of the scenery. Bierstadt took his studies back to his studio and from 1872 to 1887 used them as inspiration to produce grandly scaled oil paintings of Farallon Islands scenes. (Museum of Fine Arts, Boston.)

FARALLON ISLANDS LIGHTHOUSE, 1859. Artist Hartman Bache (1798–1872) was a lighthouse engineer who participated in the construction of many of the earliest lighthouses on the West Coast. He was also the great-grandson of Benjamin Franklin. His 1859 painting of Southeast Farallon Island depicts the Stonehouse at the base of Tower Hill, the island's lighthouse, and two men with rifles. (SCIF.)

FARALLONES ISLANDS BY JULIAN RIX, 1887. This photogravure by American artist Julian Rix (1850–1903) was published in John Muir's *Picturesque California* (page 356) in 1887. Rix had moved to San Francisco from Vermont in his youth. Largely self-taught, he became a well-known California artist, noted for his landscape paintings. Rix also contributed illustrations to *Harper's Magazine*. (SCIF.)

Two

Egging and the Southeast Farallon Egg War

The Common Murre, Lithograph by John Gould, William Hart, and H.C. Richter, 1862. The penguin-like Common Murre is the most abundant seabird that nests along the north and central California coast, including the Farallones. On the Farallon Islands, murres nest in spectacularly dense colonies on cliffs and slopes, with neighboring birds often touching each other. Murres incubate their one egg with their feet holding the egg in place. (New York Public Library.)

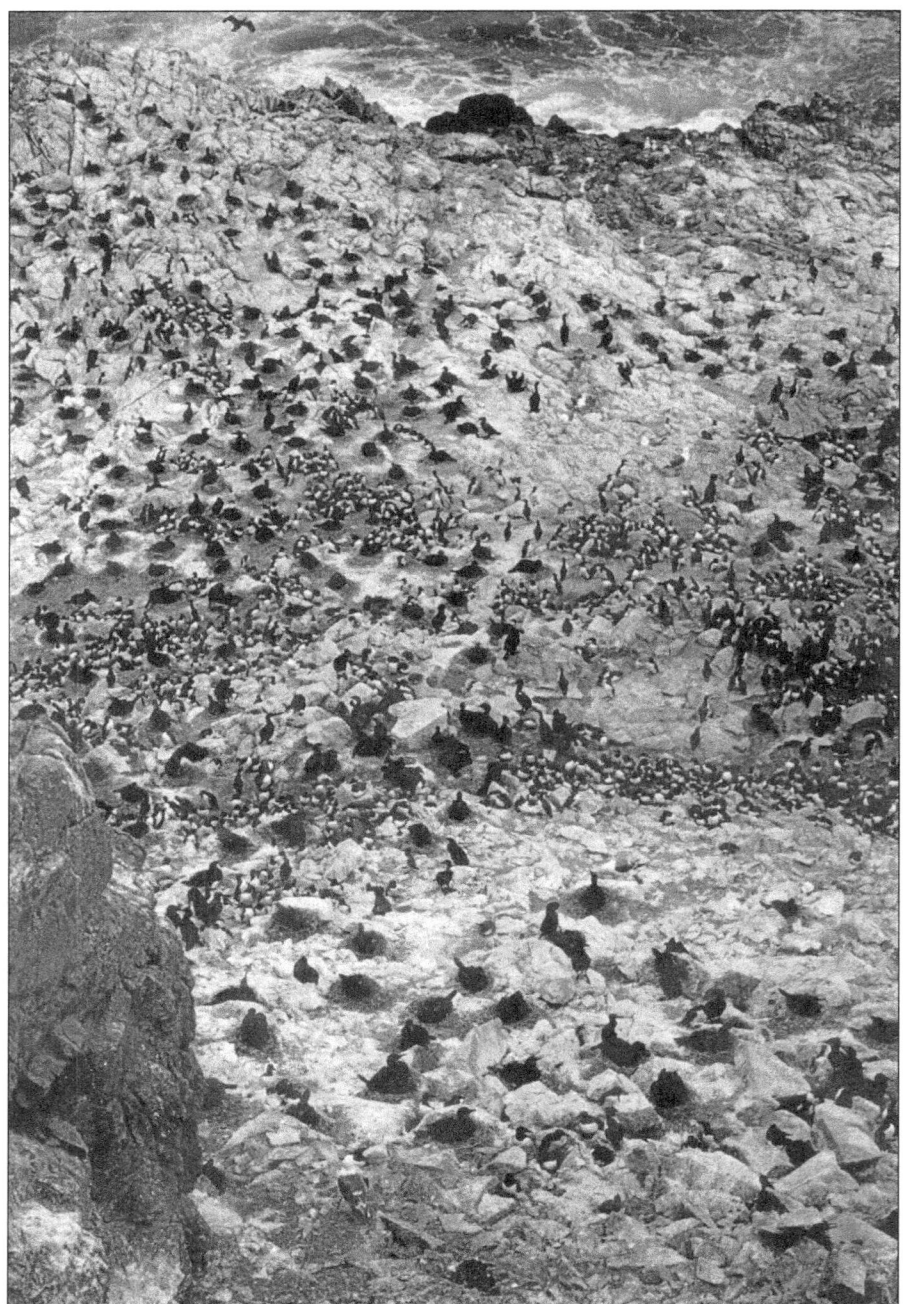

CORMORANTS NEST AMONG THE GREAT MURRE ROOKERY. There were no chickens in San Francisco during the Gold Rush, so eggs were uncommon and pricey. In 1848, "Doc" Robinson and his brother-in-law ventured to the Farallones, collected wild murre eggs, and made $3,000 for their efforts on their one and only trip. Others soon caught onto this new "egg rush," and in 1855 a group of men incorporated the Farallon Egg Company, intending to monopolize the murre egg trade, although independent pickers continued their egging activities until the end of the century. (Point Blue.)

EGG-PICKERS AT NORTH LANDING, SOUTHEAST FARALLON. Each season, egg collectors would come ashore at North Landing, where there were steps for use at high tide, ropes and a derrick for hoisting goods, and a davit for lifting a skiff. At low tide, skiffs could land on a little beach at the head of the inlet. It is reported that by 1856 between three and four million eggs had been taken. (Stereographic card by Enno Nesemann; CSL.)

EGG SCHOONER, FISHERMAN'S BAY. In the 1850s, conflicts arose over egg collecting rights, with the Farallon Egg Company claiming exclusivity. In 1863, the conflicts between rival egging companies over collecting rights escalated into violence—dubbed the "Great Egg War"—and two people were killed. (SCIF.)

SHIPPING THE MURRE EGGS, NORTH LANDING, SOUTHEAST FARALLON, C. 1867. Once the pickers had filled their egg baskets, the baskets were covered with weeds and stones to keep the gulls from pilfering the contents. The baskets were stored in a stone egg house at North Landing until the ship came in to pick them up. (Photograph by Carleton Watkins; J. Paul Getty Museum.)

GATHERING OF THE EGGS OF THE MURRE, C. 1871. Ten to 20 men, many of whom were Greek or Italian, spent from late spring through summer on Southeast Farallon collecting hundreds of dozens of eggs every season. Each year when the eggers returned, they smashed all eggs to ensure that new clutches were not hardset. The island was divided into sections, which were covered by the egg collectors every other day. (Photograph by Eadweard Muybridge; CSL.)

SCOTTIE THE EGGER, SOUTHEAST FARALLON ISLAND, JULY 1896. Each collector wore a specialized custom "egg shirt" made of cotton flour sacking with holes cut for head and arms, and with a slip down the front into which the eggs were dropped. The garment was tied tightly around the waist to form a carrier for 18 to 20 dozen eggs. Pant legs were bound at the ankle with cords to keep them from catching on rocks, and shoes were soled with plaited rope instead of leather, to give a firm grip on the island's wet, steep shale slopes. (Photograph by Arthur Bolton; CAS.)

EGG-PICKERS, SOUTHEAST FARALLON ISLAND, C. 1875. The three seated egg-pickers, with their pants legs tied at the ankles, are wearing their egging shirts full of murre eggs. Full shirt-loads of gathered eggs were transferred to large baskets. Egg baskets could hold up to 13 dozen eggs —more than 150 eggs each. On higher ground, ropes were used, and it was not uncommon for eggers to fall from narrow ledges. At least two of them died from such mishaps, and a light keeper was badly hurt. (Photograph by Chester Barlow; SCIF.)

THE ROBBERS OF THE FARALLONES. From a common base, the eggers set off together each morning along well-beaten tracks, and on arriving at the area to be collected, they spread out and began climbing over the rocks, gathering eggs as quickly as possible. Each man was followed by an umbrella of screaming western gulls, eager to steal the murre eggs from the pickers. (Photograph by Carleton Watkins; J. Paul Getty Museum.)

A Group of Men Cleaning a Week's Haul of Seabird Eggs. Eggs were washed and cleaned at North Landing near the stone egg-storage house. Packed baskets of eggs were then stored in the cool stone room to await shipment to San Francisco. There was a particularly high demand for Farallon eggs from restaurants and bakeries. (Photograph by Arthur Bolton; CAS.)

A Heap of California Murre Eggs, c. 1885. Photographer William Otto Emerson (1856–1940) was one of the foremost pioneer ornithologists of California. He moved to the state in 1870 from his home near Chicago and began his fieldwork along the coast in about 1880, making at least five trips to the Farallones between 1881 and 1887. In 1893, he was one of the founders of the Cooper Ornithological Club. Emerson's collection of 6,000 species of western birds was donated to the California Academy of Sciences. (Photograph by W. Otto Emerson; CAS.)

GROUP OF EGGERS ON SOUTHEAST FARALLON, 1892. Murre pairs gathered shoulder to shoulder on every available space to breed and incubate their one egg. When pickers robbed them of their egg, the incensed murres pecked the men's hands bloody. If the murres were successfully repelled, thieving gulls swept in to rob the unguarded eggs. (Chester Barlow Collection; MVZ.)

CROSSING THE JORDAN CHANNEL. The west end of Southeast Farallon is separated from the larger occupied portion of the island by a surge passage known as the Jordan Channel. In the early egging years, a number of devices were installed over time to cross the gap, including a breeches buoy. (CAS.)

CROSSING ON THE TROLLEY, C. 1897. A breeches buoy—a crude, rope-based rescue device normally used to extract people from wrecked vessels—was used to allow eggers to cross this sea stream channel. It is similar to today's zip line. (Chester Barlow courtesy *Overland Monthly*; SCIF.)

BRIDGE OVER JORDAN, C. 1897. Through the years, the watery gap of the Jordan Channel, joining Southeast Farallon Island to its West End, has been spanned by breeches buoys, ropes and cables, a swinging bridge, and a number of more substantial bridges, allowing egg-pickers access to heavy concentrations of nesting murres. (Chester Barlow, courtesy *Overland Monthly*; SCIF.)

CHESTER BARLOW AT A PETREL NEST, 1880s. By 1881, there had been so much trouble with the Pacific Egg Company that it was deemed necessary to eject its 11 men from the island. In May, the government steamer *Manzanita* took out a US marshal and 20 soldiers to execute the eviction and tear down their huts. Ornithologist Chester Barlow (1874–1902) made at least five collecting trips to the Farallones. (Chester Barlow Collection; MVZ.)

WILFRED H. OSGOOD COLLECTING EGGS AND BIRDS, 1892. New York–born Wilfred Hudson Osgood (1875–1947) moved in 1888 to California, where he became interested in ornithology. In the 1890s, he made several trips to the Farallones. In 1899, Osgood was graduated from Stanford University. He received his PhD in 1918 from the University of Chicago. From 1909 to 1940, Osgood was assistant curator, then curator of mammalogy and ornithology at the Field Museum of Natural History, Chicago. (Photograph by Chester Barlow; SCIF.)

SACKS OF GUANO AWAITING SHIPMENT, SOUTHEAST FARALLON, 1897. Throughout the last half of the 19th century, guano was harvested from the Farallones as a rich and valuable fertilizer. On November 13, 1857, the *Sonoma County Journal* noted the "very excellent quality of guano found on the Islands. The guano is found in crystalized lumps, and contains a large proportion of ammonia. It is found in grottos or caverns, in inexhaustible beds, and promises to prove an incomputable source of riches to the company." With the development of chemical fertilizers, the guano industry all but disappeared. (Photograph by Chester Barlow; SCIF.)

EGGERS' SHED AT NORTH LANDING, C. 1869. The egg house, built of low, mortarless stone walls, was used for storing murre and western gull eggs before shipment to San Francisco. At the close of each day's egg collecting, the full baskets were taken to the shed at North Landing, where the eggs were washed in salt water to remove stains. Feluccas came two or three times a week to pick them up. In the city, the eggs were boxed and sent to market. (Photograph by Carelton Watkins; J. Paul Getty Museum.)

EGGERS' SHED STONE RUINS AT NORTHEAST LANDING, 2017. Southeast Farallon egg collecting continued in great earnest from 1848 until enough chickens had arrived in the Bay Area some 25 years later, with the growth in the chicken industry in Petaluma starting in 1875. In 1881, the federal government removed all egging companies from the Farallon Islands, although murre egg-taking continued in declining numbers through the century. (Photograph by Bill Dewey; SCIF.)

Three

FROM KEEPERS OF THE LIGHT TO NATIONAL WILDLIFE REFUGE

SOUTHEAST FARALLON ISLAND, 1962. On February 27, 1909, Pres. Theodore Roosevelt created Farallon National Wildlife Refuge with an executive order that designated North and Middle Farallon Islands and Noonday Rock as the Farallon Reservation, establishing a "preserve and breeding ground for native birds." In 1969, the reservation became known as Farallon National Wildlife Refuge and protection was expanded to include Southeast Farallon Island. February 28, 2009, marked the 100th anniversary of the refuge. (Stanford News Service.)

FARALLON ISLAND LIGHTHOUSE, C. 1873. In 1853, the first lighthouse was constructed on Southeast Farallon's highest hill, 358 feet in elevation. The tower was torn down 18 months later when it was found to be too small to accommodate the first-order Fresnel lens. The second lighthouse was built in 1855 and modified in 1969. The Farallon Island Lighthouse was lit for the first time on January 1, 1856, by the head lighthouse keeper, Nerva Wines (1825–1901). This was the sixth lighthouse to be activated on the West Coast as a part of the Twelfth Lighthouse District. (Photograph by Eadweard Muybridge; USLHS.)

LIGHTHOUSE TOWER, C. 1878. The first-order Fresnel lens, constructed of hand-cut curved prisms set in a cast-iron frame, was shipped from France to San Francisco and installed in the rebuilt lighthouse tower in 1855. At first, the light was fueled by sperm whale oil, replaced later by lard oil, and eventually replaced by kerosene. (Photograph by Carleton Watkins; J. Paul Getty Museum.)

THE MORSE FAMILY—STEPHEN, CARRIE, AND BABY BERTHA—ON SOUTHEAST FARALLON ISLAND, C. 1873. Stephen H. Morse (1839–1879) was born in Edgartown, Massachusetts. He was a Navy veteran and lighthouse keeper on South Farallon Island. Morse initially served as first assistant lighthouse keeper (1871–1873) before being promoted to principal keeper in 1874, when keeper Joseph Macomber died. In 1875, Morse was transferred to the Piedras Blancas lighthouse. He died four years later at age 40. (Photograph by Carleton Watkins; CSL.)

FISHERMAN'S BAY, SOUTHEAST FARALLON ISLAND, 1887. In the mid-19th century, the first of two landings was developed at the northern end of Southeast Farallon Island in Fisherman's Bay. A narrow-gauge rail line with a cart to carry supplies was installed to run from the boathouse and landing to the keepers' quarters. (Photograph by Chester Barlow; SCIF.)

FARALLON LANDING FROM OCEAN SIDE, 1892. North Landing was developed in a narrow inlet at the far corner of Fisherman's Bay. A hoist was, and still is, used to lift supplies up to the landing deck atop the stone bluff. The steep ladder has since been replaced with steps cut into the rock. Landings can only be made during calm seas. (Photograph by Chester Barlow; SCIF.)

Boating Scene in Fisherman's Bay, c. 1892. At low tide, the inlet at North Landing was used recreationally by lighthouse keepers and their families for rowing and swimming activities. Small skiffs were hoisted and lowered using the derrick at the landing. (Photograph by Chester Barlow; MVZ.)

Swimming Scene in Fisherman's Bay, 1892. A small sandy cove is accessible at low tide at North Landing in Fisherman's Bay. A long, steeply angled wooden ladder ran down the rocky cliff-face from the landing above to the extremely narrow cove below. Upon closer inspection, the two young men are naked. (Chester Barlow Collection; MVZ.)

RAIL SYSTEM, SOUTHEAST FARALLON ISLAND, 1887. A narrow-gauge rail system, informally named the Farallon Midland, was installed in 1878 to connect to North Landing at Fisherman's Bay. It ran from the landing around the island's marine terrace to the residences, fog and horn station quarters, and coal storage. The line was extended to East Landing in 1896. (Photograph by W. Otto Emerson; MVZ.)

NARROW-GAUGE RAIL, VIEW LOOKING NORTHWEST, 1887. The rail cart was never motorized, but rather pulled by a burro or mule. Since the 1913 death of Patti the mule, the rail cart has been hand-pushed and pulled by the island residents. It is still used today to transport supplies to and from the landings. (Photograph by Chester Barlow; MVZ.)

FARALLON ISLAND LIGHTHOUSE, c. 1878. The Lighthouse Board, created by Congress under the Treasury Department in 1852, operated the light until it was dissolved in favor of the establishment of the Lighthouse Service (Bureau of Lighthouses) under the Department of Commerce. In 1939, the Bureau of Lighthouses was merged with the US Coast Guard, and the Coast Guard then assumed control of lighthouse operations on Southeast Farallon Island. (Photograph by Carleton Watkins; CSL.)

LIGHT KEEPERS' HOUSES, 1887. The original keepers' house, the Stonehouse on the left, was built in 1853. Between 1877 and 1881, an ambitious program of development was funded by Congress. The large Victorian houses to the right were completed by the US Coast Guard in 1878 and 1880, respectively. In his June 1887 notes, the photographer mentions, "Tufted puffin rookery is hill seen back of houses." (Photograph by W. Otto Emerson; MVZ.)

CHILDREN ON SOUTHEAST FARALLON ISLAND, 1892. There were 14 people living on Southeast Farallon Island in 1892: head keeper William Beeman and his three assistants—Cyrus J. Cain, Edward P. Cashin, and Thomas Winther; the wives of the three married men; and seven children. By 1896, ten children lived on the island. A room was outfitted as a school, with little desks, blackboards, and a supply of schoolbooks, and Miss Daisy Doud was hired at the island's first official schoolteacher. She stayed less than a year. (Chester Barlow Collection; MVZ.)

A CATCH OF ROCK COD, 1892. The waters around the various Farallones have long attracted fishermen and divers. Residents of Southeast Farallon took advantage of their access to good fishing grounds, regularly supplementing their diets with fresh-caught local fish. They sometimes traded the island's feral rabbits to fishermen for fish. (Chester Barlow Collection; MVZ.)

Lightkeepers and Their Families with Crew from the Lighthouse Tender Madroño, 1898. The 163-foot *Madroño* (1885–1927+) was designed as an inspection tender for service on the West Coast as a replacement for the tender *Shubrick*. It arrived in San Francisco, California, in January 1886. *Madroño* carried 26 officers and crewmen, and by 1890 supplied 28 light stations and 10 buoys. It also delivered the payroll for lighthouse keepers. Captain Thompson is standing in the doorway. (Bancroft Library.)

Lighthouse Tender Madroño (1885–1927+). Built in Camden, New Jersey, the 163-foot government steamer *Madroño* was launched in 1884. It was designed as an inspection tender for service on the West Coast as a replacement for the 140-foot lighthouse tender *Shubrick*, which was taken out of service in 1885. Lighthouse service tenders were the most important link to the outside world for island residents. (Mariners' Museum.)

ERNEST WINTHER (KEEPER'S SON), CHARLES A. LOVE, AND MILTON SMITH RAY IN RABBIT CAVE, 1904. Ray, Love, and photographer Oluf J. Heineman visited Southeast Farallon Island in May 1904, traveling aboard the 46-foot *Jennie Griffin* on her biweekly runs. Ray penned an article about their visit, "A Fortnight on the Farallones," in the ornithological journal *Auk* in October 1904. (Point Blue.)

LIGHTHOUSE KEEPER CHARLES KANEEN AND ISLAND RESIDENTS, 1904. Charles S. Kaneen (1866–1943) lived on Southeast Farallon Island with his wife and family while he served as second assistant keeper (1901–1903), first assistant keeper (1903–1905), and keeper (1905). He left for service at the Piedras Blancas lighthouse, followed by more than 25 years (1911–1936) as keeper of the Carquinez Strait Lighthouse. (Point Blue.)

WEATHER STATION, SOUTHEAST FARALLON ISLAND (1902–1913). In 1902, the US Weather Bureau installed a weather station on the western portion of the island. It included comfortable living quarters on the ground floor, with the weather observer's office above. The Navy built its own weather station on the island in 1905 with better equipment, and in 1913 the Weather Bureau closed its station. Its facility was given over to the Navy, which tore it down and built a succession of radio stations of its own. (SFPL.)

MONTHLY MAIL DELIVERY, SOUTHEAST FARALLON ISLAND, 1920. With no direct mainland communication available for personal use, the monthly mail delivery was always highly anticipated by the residents of Southeast Farallon Island. In the 1920s, that included lighthouse keepers and their families, as well as Navy personnel. (USCG.)

STONEHOUSE, SOUTHEAST FARALLON ISLAND, 1904. Keepers and their families shared living in the Stonehouse from 1854 until 1878–1880, when two new two-story New England–style duplexes were built. This included James Powers, first head keeper (1854–1855): Nerva Wines (1855–1859); Amos Clift (1859–1960); Jacob Decker (1860–1861); Thomas Tasker (1861–1871); Joseph Mccomber (1871–1873); Stephen H. Morse (1873–1874); Edward K. Barnum (1875–1878); and William Windsor (1878–1880). (Bancroft Library.)

STONEHOUSE, SOUTHEAST FARALLON ISLAND, c. 1930s. The Stonehouse was the first house built on Southeast Farallon for the Lighthouse Service. It was constructed in 1853 of native island stone. Its walls were three feet thick. Over the years, additions and improvements were made to the Stonehouse. Despite its historical significance, shortly after World War II, it was blown up by the Coast Guard as an unused, unneeded structure. (USCG.)

LIGHTHOUSE KEEPERS' HOUSES, SOUTHEAST FARALLON ISLAND, 1925. After two decades of lighthouse operations, with keepers sharing accommodations in the 1853 Stonehouse, the US Lighthouse Service built two new Victorian keepers' houses in 1878–1880. Each dwelling served as a duplex, and each originally had a second-story balcony. A narrow switchback trail behind the houses leads to the light. (USLHS.)

AERIAL VIEW OF THE COAST GUARD COMPLEX, SOUTHEAST FARALLON ISLAND, C. 1920S. Most of these buildings no longer exist. The former fog signal buildings in the left and center foregrounds are gone, as is the large coal shed at the end of the rail line spur. The tops of the two 43,000-gallon cisterns remain as a dominant feature of the landscape. Today, there is only one water tank on the hill above the keepers' quarters. (USCG.)

SUPPLY DELIVERY IN 1926. Navy radiomen and light keepers pushed and pulled the flatbed supply cart from North Landing along the island's rail system to the houses. Since the 1913 death of Patti the mule, the island's rail cart has been moved along the tracks by the manpower of island residents and visitors. The rail still serves island visitors today. (SFPL.)

SUPPLIES ON THE RAIL CART BETWEEN HOUSES, 1926. Deliveries by the lighthouse tenders were the lifeblood for island residents, with distribution of coal, supplies, provisions, mail from loved ones, and news from the outside world. In the early years, *Shubrick* visited once every three months. In 1885, *Shubrick* was replaced by the *Madroño* (1885–1927). Vessel calls and supply deliveries increased after the turn of the century, becoming monthly, every two weeks, and eventually weekly, weather permitting, by the 1950s. (SFPL.)

EAST LANDING NAVAL STATION, 1926. Between the wars, the Navy increased its presence on the island with a succession of staffed radio station personnel. Buildings were added near East Landing, on the island's southeast and leeward side, where landings are generally more favorable. Barracks (far right), family quarters (center), and other amenities were added. When World War II started, the Navy ran a secret radar station and the island's population grew to over 70. After the war, the Navy left the island, leaving only the Coast Guard residents. (USCG.)

CENSUS TAKER ON SOUTHEAST FARALLON ISLAND, 1940. Census taker Edward M. Gaffney (standing, in a double-breasted suit) poses with the Farallon residents on April 26, 1940. The 1940 census lists Navy chief radioman Harry Cunnington and his wife, Borghild; radioman William Oliver and his wife, Maggie; radioman John Wood, his wife, Lucy, and son, John Jr.; radio operator John Stevens, his wife, Mildred, and two sons, John and Ralph; medic Joseph Shireman; radioman Victor Babib; radio operator Albert Wein; and Filipino cook Abaya Victorino. (SFPL.)

AERIAL VIEW OF SOUTHEAST FARALLON AND EAST LANDING, PRE-1969. After World War II, human activity on Southeast Farallon steadily declined, and one building after another fell vacant. In accordance with a Coast Guard policy to remove unused structures, the fog signal complex and most of the buildings originally constructed to house the naval radio operators were torn down. The historic keepers' residence, the Stonehouse, was also destroyed. The lighthouse lens is still in place. (USCG.)

VIEW FROM MIROUNGA BAY, 2007. In July 1939, the Lighthouse Service was eliminated, and for the next quarter of a century, the Southeast Farallon light was given over to the US Coast Guard. In 1965, Coast Guard families were removed, leaving only six men to operate the station; in 1969, the lighthouse was modernized and automated; and in 1972, the last coast guardsman left the island. Island oversight was turned over to the US Fish and Wildlife Service. Note the missing lighthouse tower lens. (USFWS.)

ORIGINAL FRESNEL LENS FROM THE FARALLON LIGHTHOUSE. The original Fresnel lens, with its hand-cut curved prisms and sturdy cast-iron casing, was shipped from France and installed at the Farallon Lighthouse tower. On January 1, 1855, the light was lit for the first time by keeper Nerva Wines. After 115 years of shining its navigational light, the intricate Fresnel lens was removed in 1969 to make way for an automated light. The original lens is now on display at the San Francisco Maritime National Historical Park. (SFMNHP.)

SOUTHEAST FARALLON LIGHTHOUSE TOWER, 2017. The Farallon Island lighthouse was automated on September 1, 1972, after the lantern room and Fresnel lens had been removed. Coast Guard personnel remained on the island for an additional three months to make sure the automated light functioned properly. That same year, the US Fish and Wildlife Service entered into a cooperative management agreement with the nonprofit Point Reyes Bird Observatory to conduct biological monitoring. Observatory staff had been living on the island since 1968 by the time the agreement was formalized. In 2013, the nonprofit name was changed to Point Blue Conservation Science. Today, the islands' only human inhabitants are a few biologists and refuge staff. (Photograph by Bill Dewey; SCIF.)

Four

INTO THE 21ST CENTURY

SOUTHEAST FARALLON ISLAND, NATIONAL REGISTER OF HISTORIC PLACES, 1977. For two centuries, the South Farallones have seen extensive human activity, beginning as a pinniped hunting ground, a coveted egg-gathering site, a guano-collecting place, a manned Lighthouse Service and US Coast Guard light station, and a military outpost including a World War II naval station. These past activities left behind many remnants, some of which possess historic significance. Southeast Farallon Island was listed on the National Register of Historic Places as a historic district in 1977. (USCG.)

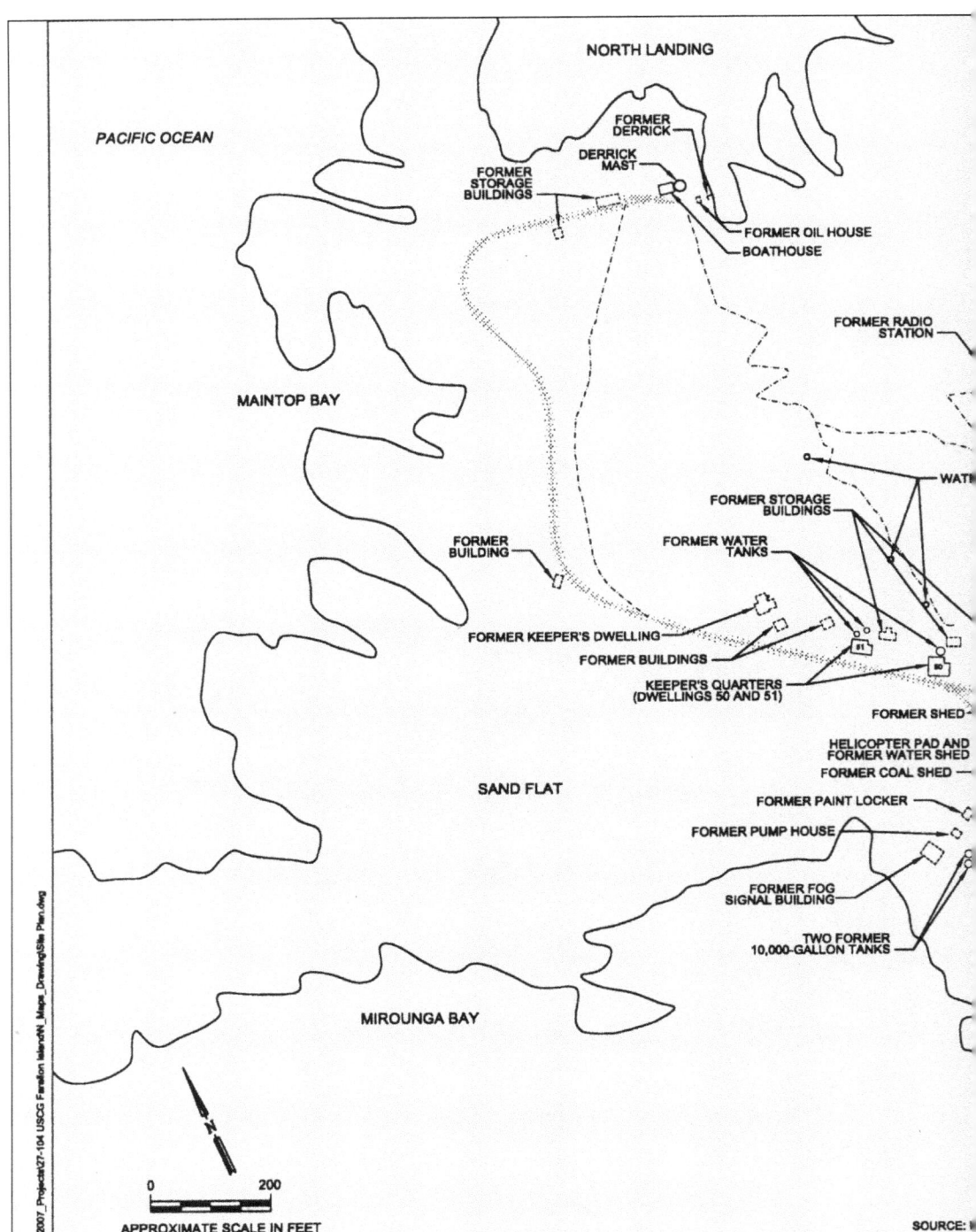

MAP OF SOUTHEAST FARALLON FORMER AND CURRENT STRUCTURES, 2009. Due to the historical nature of some of the buildings on the island that remained in the 1970s, specific features that were determined to be culturally significant include the rail cart system, the carpenter shop, the Lighthouse Hill trail with its rock walls, and the two Victorian residences, mapped as dwellings

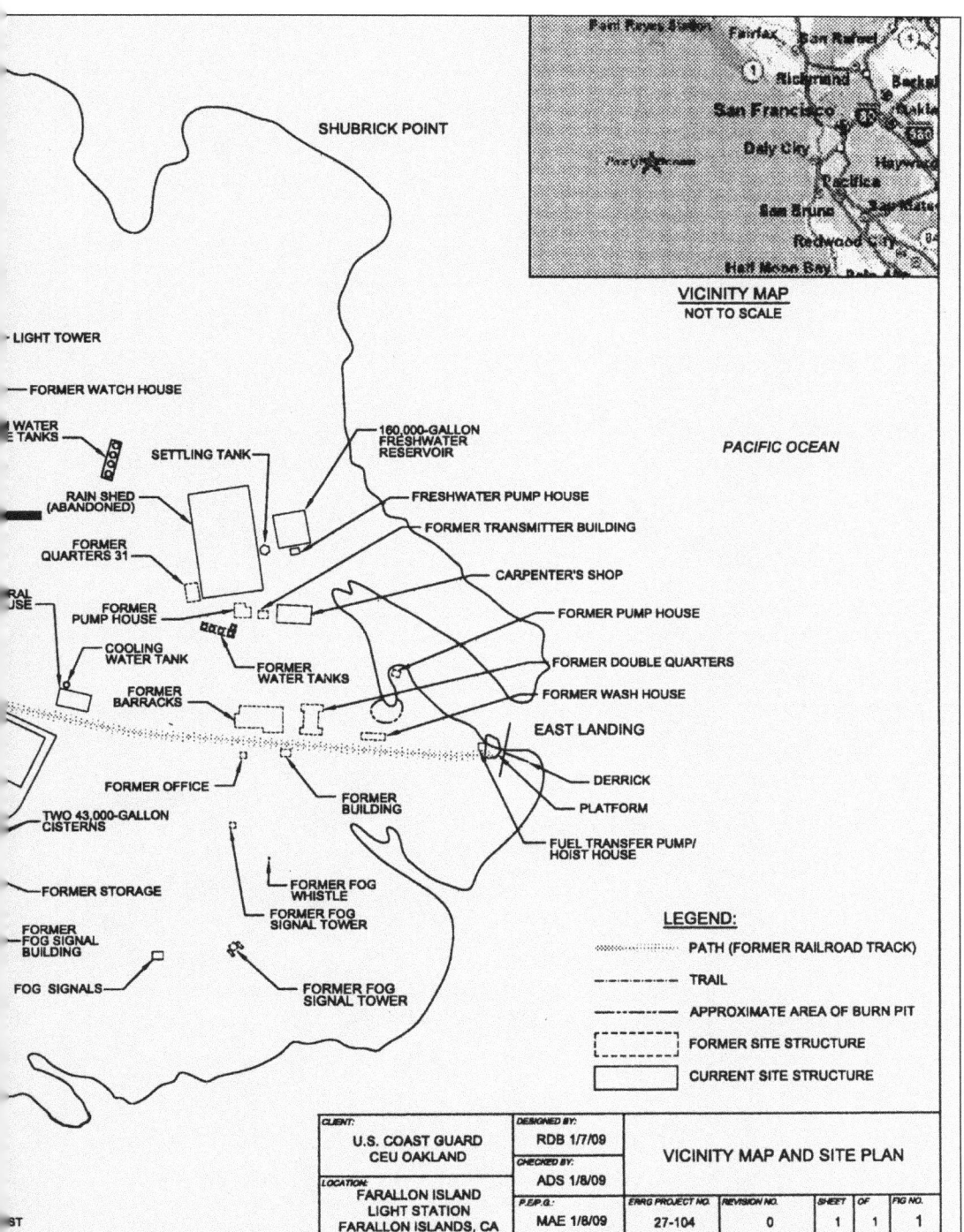

No. 50 ("Coast Guard House" on the east) and No. 51 ("PRBO House" on the west). Navy structures and other unused buildings had already been removed, including the historical Stonehouse, prior to the island's listing in the National Register. (SCIF.)

HOUSES ON SOUTHEAST FARALLON ISLAND, 2017. Originally constructed by the US Lighthouse Board in 1878–1880 to house lighthouse employees and their families, both Victorian-era houses are still serviceable today. Minor alterations have been made to both the exterior and the interior configurations. The house on the west (left foreground) is Dwelling No. 51 (PRBO House); to the east is Dwelling No. 50 (Coast Guard House). (Photograph by Bill Dewey; SCIF.)

DWELLING NO. 51, SOUTHEAST FARALLON ISLAND. Today, the Victorian house on the western side of the two dwellings, sometimes referred to as the "PRBO House," is used by staff and volunteers of Point Blue Conservation Science. Point Blue has been conducting research within the Farallon Islands National Wildlife Refuge, in close collaboration with the US Fish and Wildlife Service, since 1968. The cypress tree on the leeward side of the house, on this otherwise treeless island, is a resting destination for hundreds of species of migratory land birds. (Photograph by Bill Dewey; SCIF.)

VICTORIAN HOUSE NO. 51, SOUTHEAST FARALLON, 2017. The two nearly identical historic houses were remodeled in 1959–1962. Changes made included redesign of the front entries, balcony and chimney removal, outbuilding removal, and changes to the landscaping. Each building was converted to a single-family residence. Neither house is heated. (Photograph by Bill Dewey; SCIF.)

REAR VIEW, VICTORIAN HOUSE NO. 51, SOUTHEAST FARALLON, 2017. Former water tanks are located behind each house. The US Fish and Wildlife Service is responsible for maintenance of the island's facilities. An efficient, zero-emission custom septic system has been installed, and nearly 90 percent of the island's energy is produced through solar. (Photograph by Bill Dewey; SCIF.)

INTERIOR STAIRCASE, HOUSE NO. 51, 2017. Beautiful interior staircases connect the first and second floors of each of the houses, which are no longer configured as duplexes. Two ample-sized rooms and a kitchen occupy the first floors. Upstairs bedrooms accommodate US Fish and Wildlife staff and Point Blue biologists who monitor and document the island's avian and marine species. Special visitors and occasional Coast Guard personnel also use the houses. (Photograph by Bill Dewey; SCIF.)

REAR VIEW, VICTORIAN HOUSES, 2017. Well-defined concrete, stone-lined, and wooden pathways in front of and behind the houses lead to various parts of the island. Seabird nesting density is so thick, pathways must be used to avoid stepping on or disturbing nests, eggs, and chicks during nesting season. (Photograph by Bill Dewey; SCIF.)

CEMENT RAIN CATCHMENT SLAB, 2017. With no potable springs on Southeast Farallon Island's 95 acres, a large cement catchment was built on the island's marine terrace to capture rainwater that ran into two 43,000-gallon, dome-topped cisterns. The water was filtered and pumped into a gravity tank on the hill behind the houses. This system is abandoned. (Photograph by Bill Dewey; SCIF.)

GRAVITY TANK, SOUTHEAST FARALLON, 2017. A large wooden water tank, called the Gravity Tank, is located on the hill behind the two houses in the saddle between Little Lighthouse Hill and Lighthouse (Tower) Hill. Water was pumped up to the tank from the cistern, and the tank's elevation provided enough pressure from gravity to move the water downhill through the house pipes. The tank is no longer used. (Photograph by Bill Dewey; SCIF.)

TRAIL TO THE LIGHTHOUSE, 2017. The path to the island's highest point, Tower Hill, was carved out in 1853 to facilitate construction of the new lighthouse tower and transportation to the summit of the 73 cases that contained the lens and lantern room. After workers staged a sit-down strike, a mule named Jack was brought to the island to help pack supplies up the steep slope. The switchback trail is the only access to the lighthouse. (Photograph by Bill Dewey; SCIF.)

SOUTHEAST FARALLON CONCRETE WATER SHED COMPLEX. To provide water for the historical steam fog signal, a concrete water shed was built above the fog signal building, on the slope of the marine terrace, to catch rainwater and direct it into two round-topped, 43,000-gallon cisterns. A drain was cut through solid rock from the bottom of the cisterns to the nearest bluff. Today, the water shed is used as a helipad during the fall non-nesting season. Seal (Saddle) Rock lies offshore. (USLHS.)

SOUTHEAST FARALLON COMPLEX, 2017. The two Victorian houses are still occupied today on Southeast Farallon Island. Former storage buildings behind the houses have been removed, as have the former pump house, coal storage shed, the last of the fog signal buildings, a paint locker, and a storage shed. The central powerhouse, its roof covered in solar panels, lies to the east. (Photograph by Bill Dewey; SCIF.)

WEATHER BOX, SOUTHEAST FARALLON ISLAND. For almost half a century, Point Blue staff have taken daily readings of weather, wind, and sea surface temperature. A wire run from the weather station to the house allows wind speed and direction to be monitored from inside the house. The island's rain gauge is seen to the left. Before this, the US Coast Guard compiled the island's weather data. (Photograph by Annie Schmidt; Point Blue.)

SEAL (SADDLE) ROCK. Removal of the buildings that once occupied the fog signal complex have left the landscape with only the rounded tops of the cisterns standing out as silent testament to former times. Seal Rock offshore, so named for the preponderance of California sea lions that occupy it, is sometimes referred to as Saddle Rock. (Photograph by Annie Schmidt; Point Blue.)

RAIL CART, SOUTHEAST FARALLON ISLAND. Rail carts have been a part of the landscape on Southeast Farallon Island since 1878. Although the cart has been repaired and replaced several times over the past almost century and a half, it continues to be the most efficient way to move gear and supplies from East Landing, past the powerhouse, to the two Victorian houses. The rail tracks to North Landing are no longer viable. (Photograph by Annie Schmidt; Point Blue.)

CENTRAL POWERHOUSE, 2017. The powerhouse was built in 1944 during the Navy's occupation of the island. For decades, diesel generators ran non-stop to provide the island with power. In the late 1990s, a large solar array was installed on the building's roof, with batteries stored inside. The generators were silenced. In 2009, after a decade of service, the batteries were replaced, and in 2019, both the array and batteries were replaced. (Photograph by Bill Dewey; SCIF.)

EAST LANDING DERRICK, 1962. Off-loading people, gear, and supplies has always been problematic at Southeast Farallon. This group from Stanford University arrived on a Coast Guard vessel (standing by offshore) and was lifted ashore in a cargo basket from a shore boat (unseen) in the cove below. In the 1970s, the system was changed to a Billy Pugh net being used to lift people ashore. (Stanford News Service.)

EAST LANDING DEPARTURE. Today, at both North and East Landings, a derrick is used to lift and lower a small boat or inflatable with people and supplies arriving and departing. Over time, the landing derricks suffer saltwater corrosion and decay and must be replaced. Occasionally, waves break over the entire East Landing. (Photograph by Alan Grinberg.)

AERIAL VIEW OF SOUTHEAST FARALLON AND EAST LANDING, POST-1969. The lighthouse tower has been removed, as have all of the buildings at East Landing except the historic bunkhouse built by the Navy and today known as the carpenter shop. The four freshwater storage tanks lined up on the hill have also been removed. Several of the other Farallones can be seen to the north. (USLHS.)

CONCRETE PIERS, 2017. A small stony peak, near East Landing and to the west of the carpenter shop, was cut into to accommodate large, elevated water tanks tucked up against the hill. Today, only the foundation piers of the former tanks remain against the landscape as a reminder of times past. (Photograph by Bill Dewey; SCIF.)

VIEW FROM EAST LANDING FACING NORTH, 2017. The area surrounding East Landing was once the location of naval barracks, double quarters, large wash house, and pump house. The elevated flat area cut into the hill was the location of several water tanks. The historic carpenter shop is the only building that remains today. (Photograph by Bill Dewey; SCIF.)

CARPENTER SHOP, 2017. Today this 24-by-20-foot island-stone and wood structure, located near East Landing, is listed as a historic structure. It was built around 1905 as a bunkhouse and is the only remaining structure built by the Navy. Today, it is called the carpenter shop—one room is used for wood projects; the other is a pipe shop. The gutter above the front door is hand-carved from a single log. While the front and rear walls are 12-inch-thick stone, the east and west walls are tongue-and-groove wood. (Photograph by Bill Dewey; SCIF.)

VIEW FROM THE BACK SIDE OF THE CARPENTER SHOP, 2017. The East Landing derrick can be seen to the left, and Seal (Saddle) Rock is offshore to the right. An array of abandoned, historical water pipes are scattered about the landscape along the concrete path that leads from the cement slab rain catchment area around to the north, across the marine terrace to the houses. (Photograph by Bill Dewey; SCIF.)

EAST LANDING RAIN CATCHMENT SLAB, 2017. In about 1913, the Navy built a second freshwater collection system to the northeast of the carpenter shop, near East Landing. Water flows downhill to a settling tank, and from there is pumped through a series of filters and dumped into a 160,000-gallon, covered freshwater cistern. After decades of use, this system was abandoned when the Coast Guard began quarterly deliveries of fresh water. When Coast Guard deliveries were stopped in the late 1990s, parts of this water system were revived to serve the houses. (Photograph by Bill Dewey; SCIF.)

FRESH WATER SETTLING TANK, 2017. Both of the island's rain catchment systems were abandoned, and for years, a Coast Guard cutter pumped fresh water ashore quarterly. The eastern catchment system was revived in the late 1990s when the Coast Guard discontinued water deliveries. Because of the outside elements and guano to which rainwater is exposed, a very intensive filtration process is followed to make the water usable. Multiple treatments and filters—seven in all—are used, including GAF filters, ozonator, and ultraviolet light. An on-demand pump distributes the water. (Photograph by Bill Dewey; SCIF.)

FRESH WATER PUMP HOUSE, 2017. The pump house has a covered, 160,000-gallon cistern. Although it was abandoned during years the Coast Guard delivered fresh water, the system was revitalized by the US Fish and Wildlife Service in the late 1990s, and today serves the island's water needs. (Photograph by Bill Dewey; SCIF.)

BOATHOUSE AND BOOM AT NORTH LANDING, 2017. The ocean is so rough around Southeast Farallon that no dock or pier facility can be maintained. The two landing sites, North Landing and East Landing, are barely passable in the best of weather and seas. Each landing has a derrick to hoist dinghies. Of the two, today fewer boat landings occur at North Landing. (Photograph by Bill Dewey; SCIF.)

BOATHOUSE AT NORTH LANDING, 2017. Historically, North Landing was developed first, where a wood boathouse with a hip roof was built. The existing boathouse is much larger and supports a much stronger gable roof. Supplies landed here must be hauled by wheelbarrow to the houses, since the rails for the cart no longer run to the houses from this point. (Photograph by Bill Dewey; SCIF.)

SUN SHINING ON AULON ISLET, SOUTHEAST FARALLON, 2017. A series of scenic rock formations at the northerly end of the island form the protective barrier to the west side of Fisherman's Bay: Aulone Islet, Sea Lion Islet, Finger Rock, Arch Rock, and Sugar Loaf (out of the photograph). The word *aulon* was used in 1872 by Charles Melville Scammon when describing abalone, the mollusk gathered by Chinese fishermen. (Photograph by Bill Dewey; SCIF.)

HISTORIC AMERICAN BUILDINGS SURVEY GROUP, 2017. The Santa Cruz Island Foundation conducted a buildings and landscape documentation trip to Southeast Farallon Island in September 2017. Members pictured are, from left to right, Robert "Sandy" Bredin, Bill Dewey, Marla Daily, Kirk Connally, and Karen Blumenshine. (Photograph by Bill Dewey; SCIF.)

Five
WILDLIFE ON AND AROUND THE FARALLONES

INTRODUCED HOUSE MOUSE (*MUS MUSCULUS*). At various times, burros, mules, dogs, cats, sheep, goats, pigs, and chickens were introduced onto the island. Today, Eurasian house mice are the last remaining nonnative mammals on the island. They arrived in the 19th century, and today at upwards of 500 mice per acre, this is the highest density of a rodent known on any island in the world. Mice eat the islands' insects and spiders and compete for resources needed by the Farallon arboreal salamanders. (Photograph by Jim Tietz; Point Blue.)

Jerry the Burro Dressed for Work. Jerry arrived on the island in 1873 after his predecessor of 18 years, Jack the mule, died. Jerry's tasks included packing the oil up the steep switchback trail to the lighthouse lamp. He carried two 5-gallon cans on each side of his packsaddle—about 144 pounds. He also had to turn the windlass that pulled the rope that hauled coal and heavy articles up onto the platform at North Landing. Jerry quickly learned to run and hide when he heard the steamer's whistle approaching. (Photograph by Carleton Watkins; CSL.)

Jerry the Burro, Southeast Farallon. By the time he died in 1892, Jerry the burro was the lengthiest inhabitant of the island. It was said he knew more about weather signs than any person, and he acted as a barometer. From 12 to 24 hours before a storm, he would announce it by showing great excitement, standing with his nose facing the direction of the oncoming storm, and snorting violently. He sometimes took shelter in the coal shed. (Photograph by Carleton Watkins; J. Paul Getty Museum.)

PATTI THE MULE, 1897. Named for opera singer Adelina Patti, this mule arrived on Southeast Farallon on July 12, 1892, on the steamer *Madroño* when she was five years old. Like her predecessor Jerry the burro, Patti soon connected the steamer whistle to hard work. When supplies arrived at the landing, Patti was nowhere to be found. Keepers soon learned to capture her in advance of an expected delivery. (Photograph by Chester Barlow; SCIF.)

EUROPEAN RABBIT (*ORYCTOLAGUS CUNICULUS*), 1962. Rabbits are thought to have been introduced to Southeast Farallon sometime around 1856 by the first lighthouse keepers. Their preferred foods consisted of the native maritime goldfields and maritime sandspurry. In 1896, it was reported there were so many starving rabbits in the island that they had taken to tide pools to hunt for crabs and dead fish. The last of the rabbits was removed in 1974. (Stanford News Service.)

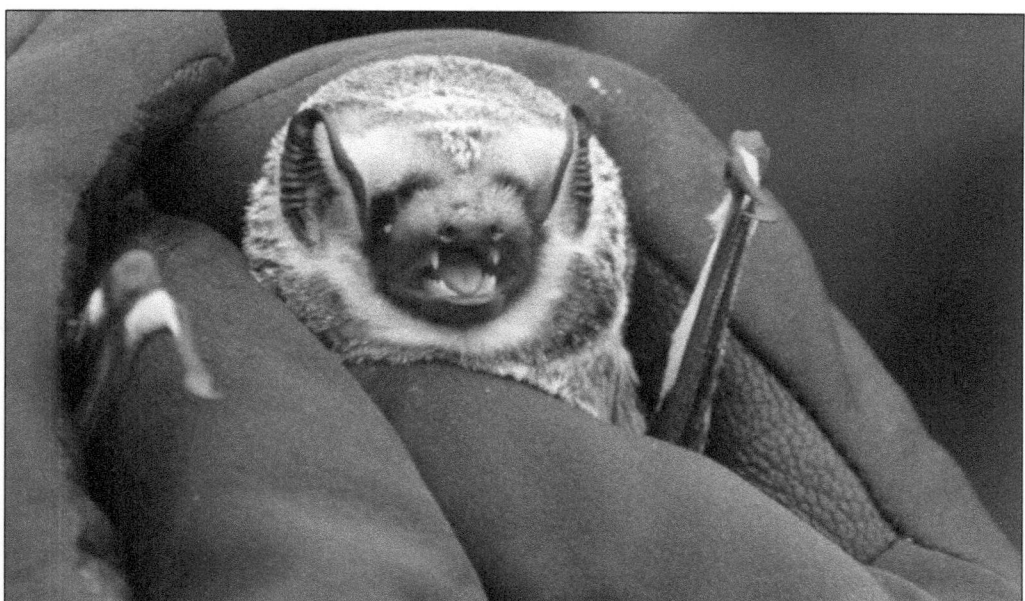

HOARY BAT (*LASIURUS CINEREUS*). Migratory bat monitoring on Southeast Farallon Island has identified five species of bats that transit the area. Hoary bats are the most frequent. They are often observed roosting in the cypress trees and mallow plants from late August through October during fall migration. Occasionally, they are also found using rock outcrops, buildings, and small caves as roosts. Hoary bats tend to live solitary lives except during migration. (Photograph by Dan Maxwell; Point Blue.)

ENDEMIC FARALLON ARBOREAL SALAMANDER (*ANEIDES LUGUBRIS FARALLONENSIS*). An insular population of arboreal salamanders, found on both Southeast Farallon and Maintop Islands, is the only amphibian found on the Farallones. It is classified as an endemic subspecies due to the distinct spot pattern and coloration as compared with mainland forms. They were first collected in 1899 by the German entomologist Charles Fuchs (1839–1914). His specimens were lost in the 1906 San Francisco earthquake and fire that destroyed the California Academy of Sciences. (Photograph by Dan Maxwell; Point Blue.)

ENDEMIC FARALLON CAMEL (CAVE) CRICKET (*FARALLONOPHILUS CAVERNICOLUS*). Species in this group are wingless and have a brownish, humpbacked appearance with large hind legs and long antennae. This endemic cricket has several anatomical features that are sufficiently distinct to warrant naming it a unique genus. The type specimen was found in a sea cave 50 feet above sea level on the southwest face of Southeast Farallon Island near the generator housing. It was first described in 1972. (Photograph by Rory Stansbury; Point Blue.)

STONE BLIND, SOUTHEAST FARALLON ISLAND, 2008. Five species of pinnipeds breed on Southeast Farallon Island: northern elephant seals, California sea lions, Steller sea lions, northern fur seals, and harbor seals. Biologists often use blinds such as this one used to view fur seals, to observe wildlife activity without causing disturbance. (Photograph by William T. Everett.)

NORTHERN FUR SEALS (*CALLORHINUS URSINUS*). Extirpated from the islands by sealers by the mid-19th century, northern fur seals have made a comeback on the Farallones. Between 1974 and 1995, one hundred eighty-one individuals were recorded, with breeding occurring as of 1996. Tagged fur seals from San Miguel Island began to appear, and pups were evident by the late 1990s. The colony has been expanding ever since. (Photograph by Oliver James; Point Blue.)

PACIFIC HARBOR SEAL (*PHOCA VITULINA*). Harbor seals can often be spotted on rocks near the water's edge with their heads and flippers elevated and being warmed by the sun. They can easily be distinguished from sea lions because they lack external ears. When harbor seals move, they drag their hind flippers behind, unlike sea lions that use their hind flippers for walking. Harbor seals can live for about 40 years. (Photograph by Annie Schmidt; Point Blue.)

CALIFORNIA SEA LIONS (ZALOPHUS CALIFORNIANUS). In the early 1800s, California sea lions were heavily hunted and extirpated from the Farallones. Two centuries later, they are the dominant of five pinniped species found on the Farallones. Here, they breed and haul out and are present year-round. California sea lions are one of the primary food sources for great white sharks. (Photograph by Steve Munch; SCIF.)

THE EMPEROR'S BATHTUB, SOUTHEAST FARALLON ISLAND, 2011. Elephant seals and California sea lions often frolic in this naturally formed deep stone pool. Cascading waterfalls created by high tides refill the pool over the tops of the surrounding rocks. (Photograph by Annie Schmidt; Point Blue.)

STELLER SEA LIONS (*EUMETOPIAS JUBATUS*). These largest of all sea lions are one of five species of pinnipeds that breed on the South Farallones. They gather in breeding groups at both Sea Lion Cove and on Seal (Saddle) Rock. Steller sea lions were listed as an endangered species in 1990, after the population declined by half between the 1960s and 1989. (Photograph by Ron LeValley; Point Blue.)

NORTHERN ELEPHANT SEALS AND CALIFORNIA SEA LIONS SHARING SPACE, FARALLON ISLANDS NATIONAL WILDLIFE REFUGE. The five species of seals and sea lions found at the Farallones often compete for space. California sea lions are the most abundant, and at any given time there are thousands of pinnipeds on and around the islands. Peaks of more than 10,000 animals have been observed in recent years. (Photograph © Frans Lanting.)

MALE ELEPHANT SEAL BATTLE. Elephant seals are the largest pinnipeds in the world. Adult males can weigh more than 5,000 pounds. During breeding season, alpha males do bloody battle to protect and maintain their harems. Only about a third of males win the chance to breed. (Photograph by Brent Stewart.)

NORTHERN ELEPHANT SEAL PUPS (MIROUNGA ANGUSTIROSTRIS). Elephant seals were hunted to near extinction in the 19th century. After more than a century of legal protection, colonies of elephant seals spread among the California islands. In 1959, they began recolonizing the Farallones. By 1971, over 100 juveniles were counted, and breeding began in 1972. (Photograph by Annie Schmidt; Point Blue.)

POINT BLUE BIOLOGIST RYAN BERGER, STANDING NEAR A MALE NORTHERN ELEPHANT SEAL (MIROUNGA ANGUSTIROSTRIS), 2010. Today, large numbers of elephant seals can be seen during the winter months—from December through February. They often work their way up the marine terrace to areas around the houses, particularly restless males. (Point Blue.)

COMMON DOLPHIN (*DELPHINUS* SP.). Common dolphin species range from about six to eight feet in length, with males generally being longer and heavier. They have dark backs with light-colored sides and bellies. Common dolphins often travel in aggregations of hundreds or even thousands of individuals. They do not fare well in captivity. Recent conditions around the Farallones have suited this warmer-water cetacean. (Photograph by Richard Jackson.)

PACIFIC WHITE-SIDED DOLPHIN (*LAGENORHYNCHUS OBLIQUIDENS*). These dolphins keep close company and swim in groups of 10 to 100 or more. They can often be seen bow-riding and doing somersaults. Members form a close-knit group and will often care for a sick or injured dolphin. Young dolphins communicate with a touch of a flipper as they swim beside adults. (Photograph by Giancarlo Thomae; SCIF.)

RISSO'S DOLPHIN (*GRAMPUS GRISEUS*). These blunt-headed dolphins typically can be seen off the Farallones in groups of a few animals to perhaps 30 individuals. They bear lots of scars, made by the teeth of their own kind or by the beaks of their preferred prey, squid. Grampus, as they are often called, are one of the largest species of dolphins. They dwell over deep water in order to hunt migrating squid. (Photograph by Giancarlo Thomae; SCIF.)

KILLER WHALES (*ORCINUS ORCA*) CIRCLING A SEAL AT SOUTHEAST FARALLON ISLAND, 2012. In addition to dolphins and porpoises, the waters surrounding the Farallones are home to many diverse species of whales. Toothed whale species in the area include pilot and killer whales, and occasionally sperm whales. Killer whales often dine on seals and sea lions, although they are also known to eat seabirds. They are the only predators of great white sharks. (Photograph by James Moskito.)

HUMPBACK WHALE (MEGAPTERA NOVAEANGLIAE). Baleen whale species sighted near the Farallones include humpback, gray, finback, minke, and the largest of all whale species, the blue whale. Generally, humpback whales can be seen from mid-May to mid-September. They are often seen breeching out of the water, performing aerobatic leaps. (Photograph by Richard Jackson.)

HUMPBACK WHALE AND SEA LION OFF SOUTHEAST FARALLON. The nutrient-rich waters of the Greater Farallones National Marine Sanctuary provide sustenance for a multitude of marine species. The California Current and Eastern Pacific Upwelling fill and renew the waters with phytoplankton that forms the base of a large food web that in turn attracts and supports a large and complex ecosystem. (Photograph by Annie Schmidt; Point Blue.)

GRAY WHALE (*ESCHRICHTIUS ROBUSTUS*). The Farallones are on the travel route for several whale species. Gray, humpback, and blue whales are the most common. Gray whales migrate 10,000 miles each year, from feeding grounds in the Bering Sea to calving lagoons in Baja California and back. They transit past the Farallones in the winter headed south, and again in the spring headed north with their newborn calves. (Photograph by Richard Jackson.)

BLUE WHALE (*BALAENOPTERA MUSCULUS*). Blue whales live in all oceans of the world. They range from about 80 to 100 feet in length, and have a general cruising speed of 5 miles per hour, but they can accelerate up to 20 miles per hour when needed. Surprisingly, they are the loudest animals on the planet. Their sounds can reach 188 decibels. (Photograph by Richard Jackson.)

BLUE WHALE (*BALAENOPTERA MUSCULUS*). Blue whales are filter feeders. Instead of teeth, they have 300 to 400 fringed baleen plates that hang from their upper jaws and strain their food. They eat krill, a small shrimplike invertebrate found in colder waters. (NOAA.)

Five

EXTRAORDINARY SEABIRDS

JACK SWENSON TAGGING A MIST-NETTED BIRD, 1983. Since the late 1960s, Point Reyes Bird Observatory (renamed Point Blue) has conducted daily bird monitoring and tagging of migratory species, and to date over 430 species have passed through. The island's lack of vegetation is not conducive to attracting resident nesting species. (Photograph by Joe Kennedy; SCIF.)

SEABIRD HAVEN, SOUTHEAST FARALLON ISLAND, 2012. An amazing number of seabird species nest on Southeast Farallon—upwards of 350,000 individuals—along with one shorebird, the black oystercatcher. Between March and August, 12 species of seabirds currently nest on the Farallones: ashy storm-petrels; Leach's storm-petrels; Cassin's auklets; rhinoceros auklets; pigeon guillemots; common murres; tufted puffins; double-crested, Brandt's, and pelagic cormorants; western gulls; and California gulls. (Photograph by Ron LeValley; Point Blue.)

ASHY STORM-PETREL (OCEANODROMA HOMOCHROA). The Ashy Storm-Petrel is a scarce seabird common only within its range off California and northwestern Baja California, Mexico. The species relies upon the isolated breeding grounds of the Farallones, its largest colony, as well as several California Channel Islands, where it nests in rock crevices along cliffs, in offshore rocks, and under driftwood in sea caves. Half the world's population of ashy storm-petrels nest at the Farallones. They are a nocturnal species. (Photograph by David Pereksta.)

LEACH'S STORM-PETREL (*OCEANODROMA LEUCORHOA*). This small seabird, named after the British zoologist William Elford Leach (1791–1836), is found in both the Atlantic and Pacific Oceans. At the Farallones, these are far less common than Ashy storm petrels. Unlike its dark-feathered relative, the Leach's storm-petrel is dark with a white rump. They nest out of sight in cavities or burrows on the upper slopes of Tower Peak. (Photograph by Steve Young.)

CASSIN'S AUKLET (*PTYCHORAMPHUS ALEUTICUS*). This compact seabird, named for Pennsylvania naturalist John Cassin (1813–1869), is a colonial nester. The bird digs burrows by using its strong legs, sharp claws and beak, and in suitable ground, its burrow may be two meters long. In the Farallon talus and rock, the birds use any suitable cavity. Cassin's auklets are strictly nocturnal. (Photograph by Jack Swenson.)

RHINOCEROS AUKLET (CERORHINCA MONOCERATA). In the early 1970s, this species reestablished a breeding population on Southeast Farallon after an absence of a century. Like Cassin's auklets, rhinoceros auklets are nocturnal. (Photograph by Ron LeValley; Point Blue.)

PIGEON GUILLEMOT (CEPPHUS COLUMBA). These very rare seabirds are dramatically colored. In breeding plumage, they are jet black, with bold white patches on the upper surface of the wings and bright red legs, feet, and mouth lining. Pigeon guillemots are summer nesters that lay eggs in shallow cavities in the gradually sloped talus of the South Farallones. They tend to stay in small, loose colonies. Both parents incubate a single egg, and successful chicks usually return to their natal colony to breed. Pigeon guillemots dive into the water to feed on fish and invertebrates. (Photograph by Ron LeValley; Point Blue.)

TUFTED PUFFIN (*LUNDA CIRRHATA*). Common residents and breeders on Southeast Farallon, tufted puffins are striking in appearance. They are tar black with a red bill and feet. Their face is white with large white head tufts. They are present on the island from mid-March to early September. Eggs are laid in early May. Incubation of a pair's single egg is 45 days. The Farallon Islands lie at the southern extreme of the tufted puffin breeding range. They were much more numerous in the 19th century than they are now. (Photograph by Ron LeValley; Point Blue.)

COMMON MURRE (*URIA AALGE*). These beautiful black-and-white, penguin-like birds are not very agile on land, but in the water they are far more agile. They are abundant resident breeders on Southeast Farallon, where they breed in high-density colonies and outnumber all other species combined. Cormorants nest among the murres. (Photograph by Ron LeValley; Point Blue.)

Pair of Common Murres with Their Single Egg. In the first half of the 19th century, Russians not only harvested murre eggs but also killed the birds for feathers and meat. During the second half of the 19th century, common murre eggs were commercially harvested for the San Francisco market. It is estimated that between 1848 and 1856, more than three million eggs were taken. By the early 20th century, the population of common murres had necessarily dramatically declined. (Photograph by Annie Schmidt; Point Blue.)

MURRE AND CHICK. If murres are flushed, gulls swoop down on their nests taking either egg or chick. Murres defend against intrusion with their stiletto-like bill. Egg-gatherers often had bloodied hands from stealing murre eggs. (Photograph by Annie Schmidt; Point Blue.)

CORMORANTS, MURRES AND GULLS AT SEA LION COVE, SOUTHEAST FARALLON ISLAND. Three species of cormorants nest on the Farallones: Brandt's, pelagic, and double-crested. The Brandt's cormorant is the biggest and most abundant of the three, and in most years the Farallones host the largest breeding colony of this species in the world. (Photograph by Ron LeValley; Point Blue.)

BRANDT'S CORMORANT (*PHALACROCORAX PENICILLATUS*) CARRYING NESTING MATERIALS. In the spring months, cormorants and gulls collect maritime goldfields, locally known as Farallon weed, for ground nest building material. This native maritime plant dominates the spring landscape on Southeast Farallon. (Photograph by Annie Schmidt; Point Blue.)

Brandt's Cormorants Courting on Southeast Farallon Island. Birds begin to arrive in mid to late March; the population peaks in late May. Adults do not leave their nests and young unattended because western gulls would steal their eggs and chicks. The majority of the colony departs by late August. (Photograph by Annie Schmidt; Point Blue.)

DOUBLE-CRESTED CORMORANT (*PHALACROCORAX AURITUS*). This cormorant species is the most widespread cormorant in North America. This large waterbird has a long tail and neck. Breeding birds have small tufts on the side of the head and orange-yellow skin around the base of the bill and chin. From 300 to 400 of these cormorants breed in one colony on the Farallon Islands each year. (Photograph by Tom Haglund.)

PELAGIC CORMORANT (*PHALACROCORAX PELAGICUS*). The pelagic cormorant, sometimes referred to as a pelagic shag, is the smallest of the three cormorant species that nest on the South Farallones. It uses its own guano to solidify its nest materials and to cement its nest to the cliff face. As many as 800 pelagic cormorants breed on the Farallon Islands. (Photograph by David Pereksta.)

Pelagic Cormorant (*Phalacrocorax pelagicus*). The pelagic cormorant is the second-most common of the three cormorant species on Southeast Farallon. They are abundant residents and breeders, with numbers exceeding 2,000 breeding birds. Most arrive to nest from December to April. Their population generally peaks in May and June, and by September most birds have departed the island. (Photograph by Annie Schmidt; Point Blue.)

WESTERN GULL (*LARUS OCCIDENTALIS*) WITH CHICKS. The second-most conspicuous bird after the common murre, western gulls are abundant year-round residents and breeders on Southeast Farallon, with peak numbers exceeding 25,000 individuals. They actually can lack adequate nesting space. Gulls opportunistically raid nests and feed on chicks of several species. One keeper noted they kept the rabbit population in check. They are known to live up to 34 years. (Photograph by Dan Harding.)

WESTERN GULL, SOUTHEAST FARALLON ISLAND. Like most gulls, western gulls are opportunistic feeders, capturing live prey, scavenging refuse, and stealing food from other gulls and even seals and sea lions. They alert gulls and humans to pinniped births to scavenge the afterbirth, and they attend great white shark kills, stealing food. (Photograph by Scarlett Hutchin; Point Blue.)

COLLECTION OF OBJECTS INGESTED BY GULLS, SOUTHEAST FARALLON ISLAND. Gulls often ingest shiny objects, including items made of plastics and metal. This interesting collection of regurgitated items includes fragments of driver's licenses and credit cards, a key, a few toy cars, a pacifier, hard plastic LEGO blocks, marbles, a Happy Birthday balloon, and drink stirrers from a restaurant in Newport Beach and another from Denver. (Photograph by Scarlett Hutchin; Point Blue.)

CALIFORNIA GULL (*LARUS CALIFORNICUS*). This species is an abundant visitor but only a sporadic breeder on the Farallones. The smaller size and green feet of the California gull distinguish it from the pink-footed western gulls. California gulls also have red and black spots on their bills. (Photograph by Annie Schmidt; Point Blue.)

SEABIRD NESTING SEASON, 1962. Visitors to Southeast Farallon Island during nesting season are regularly bombarded by gulls protecting their nests and by seabirds dropping guano. Large colonies of different seabirds occupy the island simultaneously. Each species prefers a different type of habitat. (Stanford News Service.)

WESTERN GULL DIVING ON A RESEARCHER, SOUTHEAST FARALLON ISLAND. During nesting season, western gulls can become very territorial and aggressive in defending their nesting territory. Screaming and crying out, they are known to dive on intruders. The can easily inflict injury with their sharp beaks. (Photograph by Annie Schmidt; Point Blue.)

BLACK OYSTERCATCHER (*HAEMATOPUS BACHMANI*). The black oystercatcher is the only resident nesting shorebird on the South Farallones. Additional non-breeding shorebirds that visit the Farallones include western, least, and pectoral sandpipers; black and ruddy turnstones; short-billed and long-billed dowitchers; red-necked and red phalaropes; wandering tattlers; whimbrels; willets; killdeers; marbled godwits; and surfbirds. (Photograph by Ron LeValley; Point Blue.)

FARALLON PROGRAM BIOLOGIST PETE WARZYBOK. Now called "Old Man Farallon," Warzybok joined the Point Reyes Bird Observatory's Farallon Program as a volunteer seabird research intern in the spring of 2000. The following year, he was hired as a program biologist. Now, almost two decades later, senior marine ecologist Pete Warzybok has spent more than 2,200 days living and working on the Farallones. Biologists have maintained a continuous daily presence on the island since 1968. (Point Blue.)

Seven

PLANTS BOTH NATIVE AND INTRODUCED

J.W. BLANKINSHIP (1862–1938). Joseph William Blankinship is the first person known to have collected plant specimens on Southeast Farallon Island. He collected 11 native and 17 introduced species, and published a paper, "On the Natural History of the Farallon Islands" (1892), in the journal *Zoe*. Four years later, Blankinship received his master's degree from Harvard in 1896; he received his doctorate in biology from Harvard in 1898. His Farallon Islands plant collections were never located. (Jepson Herbaria; UCB.)

ELEPHANT SEALS HAULED OUT ON TRAMPLED GROUND, 2008. Due to the harsh environment, overall lack of soil, extensive guano deposits, and continuous trampling activity by pinnipeds and seabirds, plant species diversity is extremely low on Southeast Farallon Island. Less than 100 species of plants have been recorded, including about 45 native taxa and just over 50 nonnative species. Many are no longer found; others are occasionally accidentally introduced. Today, about 40 species grow on the island. (Photograph by William T. Everett.)

YOUNG EUCALYPTUS TREES ARRIVING ON SOUTHEAST FARALLON ISLAND, 1949. There have been multiple attempts to grow trees on this otherwise treeless island. In 1949, dozens of eucalyptus trees were planted on the windward side of Southeast Farallon in an attempt to grow a windbreak, but the unyielding wind and shallow, gravelly soil foiled the attempts. (Fred Lyon; SFPL.)

HISTORIC CYPRESS TREES IN 1920. Before 1920, a number of Monterey cypress (*Cupressus macrocarpa*) had been planted near the two lighthouse keepers' quarters. This 1920 photograph shows trees on the leeward side of one of the houses that are several years old and more than 12 feet tall. The white fence around the trees was removed in later years. (USLHS.)

MONTEREY CYPRESS IN 2008. Of the many tree-planting attempts, only four Monterey cypress trees and one Monterey pine survive. Introducing plant species to islands is no longer considered an acceptable practice, and in many cases introduced species are removed. The cypress trees are a part of the island's historic landscape. They are noninvasive, and they remain as an attractant for migrating land birds. Biologists use the areas around the trees to mist-net birds they then band. (Photograph by William T. Everett.)

NEW ZEALAND SPINACH (TETRAGONIA TETRAGONIOIDES). In 1968, seabird biologist Malcolm Coulter (1948–2013) made the first discovery of introduced New Zealand spinach on Southeast Farallon Island. It is edible and can be eaten raw or cooked. For the past several years, this species has been the target of an invasive plant removal program on the island. This nonnative species grows during the seabird breeding season and covers over important nesting areas. (Photograph by Jean Pawek.)

INTRODUCED TREE MALLOW (LAVATERA ARBOREA). There are several patches of the attractive nonnative bush mallow near the houses and on the east end of the marine terraces on Southeast Farallon Island. These introduced Mediterranean plants have not shown to be invasive, and like the introduced cypress trees, they are kept for their value to migrant land birds. They were first collected in the late 1960s by biologist Malcolm Coulter. (Photograph by Jim Tietz; Point Blue.)

MINER'S LETTUCE (CLAYTONIA PERFOLIATA). This California native annual herb can be eaten raw as a leaf vegetable in salads. The common name is said to have come from California Gold Rush miners who ate it to prevent scurvy. Miner's lettuce was one of the plants collected by Joseph Blankinship on the island in 1892. (SBBG.)

FARALLON WEED—
MARITIME GOLDFIELDS
(*LASTHENIA MARITIMA*).
Native maritime or
seaside goldfields
dominate the spring
landscape on Southeast
Farallon. The plant
was highly esteemed
by 19th-century island
residents as "greens." It
was also the plant that
sustained the island's
former rabbit population.
(Photograph by Oscar
Johnson; Point Blue.)

FARALLON WEED IN THE SPRING, SOUTHEAST FARALLON ISLAND. After the first spring rains, Farallon weed dominates the landscape and covers much of the island. Peak vegetative growth and flowering (March–April) coincides with the beginning of the seabird-breeding season. Cormorants and gulls collect the plant for ground nest building material. The senesced plant debris is utilized as hiding cover for gull chicks. (USFWS.)

SEASIDE DAISY (*ERIGERON GLAUCUS*). This perennial daisy is native to California and Oregon, where it is found along mainland and island coastlines. Showy flowers have yellow centers with petals of deep blue and purple to nearly white. On the Farallones, seaside daisies and their showy flowers fill crevices on sheer rock walls (Photograph by Steve Junak; SBBG.)

WHITE-TIP CLOVER (*TRIFOLIUM VARIEGATUM*). This annual native clover is one of four species of clover that has been found on Southeast Farallon Island. The others are bull clover (*Trifolium fucatum*), small-headed clover (*Trifolium microcephalum*), and the introduced Italian clover (*Trifolium incarnatum*). (SBBG.)

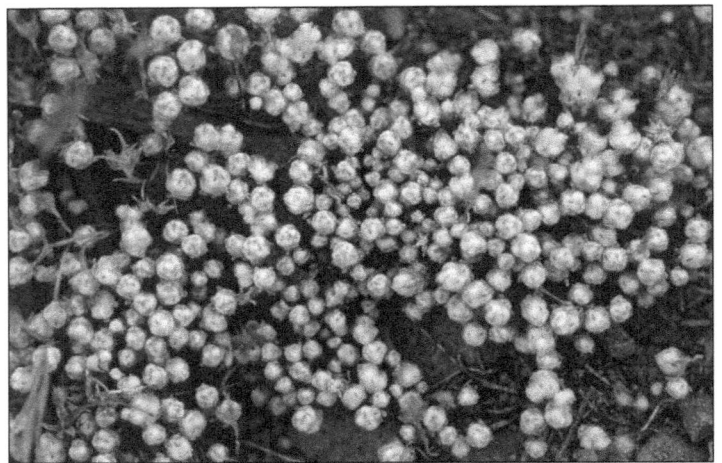

SLENDER WOOLY-MARBLES (*PSILOCARPHUS TENELLUS*). This native low-growing annual in the sunflower family is another of the plants first collected on the island by Joseph Blankinship in 1892. The tiny clustered flower heads are covered with thick woolly fibers, making them appear cottony. (SBBG.)

TORREY'S SURFGRASS (*PHYLLOSPADIX TORREYI*). This surfgrass is a native California monocot, and one of only a few species of flowering plants found in the marine waters of the North Pacific. Surfgrass grows in rocky beds in the surf zone around the Farallon Islands. When exposed during low tides, its long slender shiny green leaves can be seen clinging to rocks. Surfgrass provides habitat for many invertebrate and algae species as well as a nursery habitat for fish. (Photograph by Gerald D. Carr.)

Eight

THE DEVIL'S TEETH ARE A HAZARD TO NAVIGATION

AERIAL APPROACH TO SOUTHEAST FARALLON ISLAND. Dozens of vessels, from major ships to small sailboats, have met their end at the Farallon Islands. Large vessels lost in the 20th century include the five-masted schooner *Louis* (1907); 170-foot Navy tugboat USS *Conestoga* (1921); and the Liberty ship SS *Henry Bergh* (1944). (Photograph by Jack Swenson.)

Fog Signal, 1969. Even with the lighthouse in operation, in 1858, the three-masted ship *Lucas* foundered on the island during dense fog, prompting the call for a fog signal. The first one installed very cleverly used a naturally occurring blowhole with a whistle attached, powered by natural wave action. After it was destroyed in 1875 by high seas, a coal-fired, steam-operated fog signal replaced the blowhole whistle in 1880. In 1907, it was converted from steam to oil. In 1918, an air diaphone fog signal was installed. Diaphones became the standard from the 1920s until the early 1970s, when most lighthouses were automated. In 1970, the fog signal was taken out of service. (USLHS.)

STORM AT EAST LANDING. Of all the Devil's Teeth, only Southeast Farallon Island is accessible by boat, and only during relatively calm seas. There are two possible landing areas, each with derricks to hoist skiffs and supplies: North Landing and East Landing. Only Southeast Farallon supports historical structures, several of which are maintained for management purposes. North Farallones, Middle Farallon, and Noonday Rock are inaccessible by boat. (Photograph by Ron LeValley; Point Blue.)

SHIPWRECK, 1890S. Large 19th-century vessels lost include the 102-foot three-masted ship *Lucas*, 23 deaths (1858); 197-foot clipper ship *Noonday* (1863); lumber schooner *Morning Light* (1868); 183-foot American clipper ship *Annie Sise* (1871); 216-foot clipper ship *Champlain*, 2 deaths (1875); 205-foot three-masted sailing ship *Franconia* (1881); fishing vessel *Pirate*, 5 deaths, including *Farallon* lighthouse keeper W.C. Partlow (1881); 328-foot three-masted iron screw steamer *Bremen* (1882); lumber schooner *American Boy* (1890); and 116-foot three-masted bark *Helen W. Almy*, all 40 passengers and crew lost (1898). (Photograph by Arthur Bolton; CAS.)

PAINTING OF NOONDAY (1855–1863). On January 1, 1863, the 197-foot clipper ship *Noonday*, 139 days out of Boston, was approaching the entrance to San Francisco in clear weather and calm seas when, about eight miles west of the North Farallon, she struck a rock but glided clear. However, her bottom had been stove, and she immediately filled with water and sank in 40 fathoms. *Noonday* was lost on her fourth trip to San Francisco. (C.B. Webster & Co., *Sailing Ships of New England*.)

BELL OF THE NOONDAY. The rock that sent the *Noonday* to her grave was covered by 18 feet of water. While local pilots knew its location, the rock was not marked on navigation charts at the time. Today's charts identify it as Noonday Rock. In 1934, the trawler *Junta* found the bell of *Noonday* tangled in her nets. (SFMNHP.)

BRITISH SHIP BREMEN (1858–1882). At 1:00 a.m. on October 16, 1882, in a heavy fog during a severe swell, the 328-foot, iron-hulled ship *Bremen* struck head-on into the northwest side of Southeast Farallon Island near Seal (Saddle) Rock. Bremen was 118 days out of Liverpool, carrying a cargo of coal and whiskey. All aboard were saved in lifeboats. The island's fog signal was not working, thus the ship's captain was acquitted of negligence. (SFMNHP.)

BREMEN ANCHOR, EAST LANDING, 2017. At sunrise on October 16, 1882, the lighthouse keeper discovered the 328-foot, iron-hulled ship *Bremen* abandoned just 400 feet away from the fog whistle. Today, a large iron anchor salvaged from the ship lies at East Landing, having been placed there by salvagers. (Photograph by Bill Dewey; SCIF.)

WRECK OF THE USS CONESTOGA CONFIRMED, 2016. In 2009, a submerged wreck was discovered in the Greater Farallones National Marine Sanctuary. Seven years later, an announcement was made confirming the identification of the USS *Conestoga*, 95 years after the ship was lost. The sunken ship, graveyard to 56 men, was listed in the National Register of Historic Places in 2016. (NOAA.)

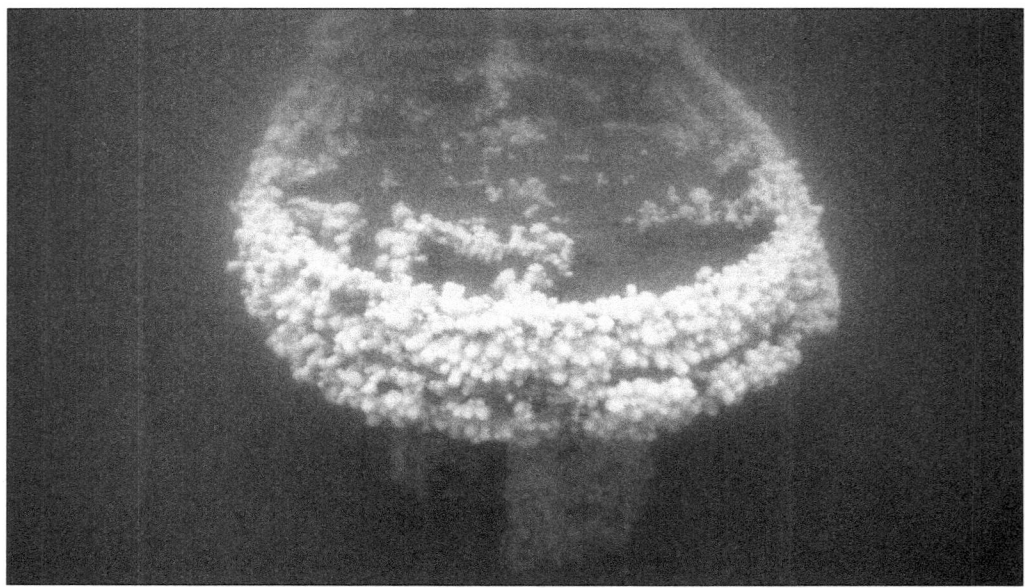

DISAPPEARANCE OF THE USS CONESTOGA, 1921. The *Conestoga* (1917–1921) was an oceangoing tug in the US Navy and purchased for use in World War 1. On March 25, 1921, with 56 men aboard, the vessel sailed out of Mare Island, 23 miles northeast of San Francisco, headed to Pearl Harbor, Hawaii, and was never heard from again. The disappearance of the USS *Conestoga* in March 1921 remained a mystery for 95 years. (NOAA.)

WRECK OF THE SS HENRY BERGH, 1944. The steamship *Henry Bergh* was an American Liberty ship chartered to the US Navy to transport soldiers returning from the war from Pearl Harbor to San Francisco. Her official capacity was 564 passengers. On May 31, 1944, overloaded with 1,300 sailors and a crew of 95, the *Henry Bergh* ran hard aground on the Drunk Uncle Islets, South Farallones. No lives were lost. (National Archives.)

LOW SPEED CHASE, 2012. On April 14, 2012, during the Full Crew Farallones Race sponsored by the San Francisco Yacht Club, the *Low Speed Chase*, a Sydney 38, was wrecked two-tenths of a mile off Maintop, Southeast Farallon. Five of the eight crew aboard were drowned. The loss is the worst tragedy in the history of Northern California offshore racing. The final wreck report determined the wreck occurred due to "a failure of seamanship." (Photograph by Sophie Webb; Point Blue.)

MYSTERIOUS DISAPPEARANCE OF JIM GRAY. On January 28, 2007, legendary and beloved Microsoft researcher and experienced sailor Jim Gray, 63, departed alone for the Farallones aboard his 40-foot fiberglass cruiser, *Tenacious*, to spread his mother's ashes. Once outside the Golden Gate, Gray called and left an upbeat message for his daughter. That was his last communication before he and his boat vanished. His mysterious disappearance, covered by national news, inspired one of the most ambitious search-and-rescue missions in history. Gray's widow had him declared missing and presumed dead in 2013. (Wikimedia Commons.)

Nine
SHARK PARK AND THE 30-MILE SWIM

GREAT WHITE SHARK (CARCHARODON CARCHARIAS) BITING A SURFBOARD AT SOUTHEAST FARALLON, 1995. Although humans are not the preferred prey of great white sharks, it is estimated that 40 percent of all shark attacks in the United States occur in what is known as the Red Triangle off the Farallones. Great white sharks are particularly notable for their large size. Females average 17 to 19 feet, and the smaller males average 11 to 13 feet in length. Their life span is thought to be upwards of 70 years. (SCIF.)

LOS FARALLONES ARE A GREAT WHITE SHARKS' WORLD. A roughly triangle-shaped region of the Pacific Ocean off the coast of Northern California, called the Red Triangle, is known for its concentrations great white sharks, seals, and sea lions. It extends beyond the Farallones to the west, to Bodega Bay to the north, and to Monterey in the south. Scientists refer to the area as the SOFA (Shared Off-Shore Foraging Area). (Photograph by Mark Marache.)

MALE GREAT WHITE SHARKS AT SOUTHEAST FARALLON, 2014. Every September through November, the same great white sharks return to exactly the same spot for about three months, year after year, in what is thought to be one of the world's largest and densest congregations of these top-level oceanic predators. While males return annually, females apparently may return only every other year. (Photograph by Scot Anderson.)

SCOT ANDERSON TAGGING A SHARK, 2005. In 1988, backed by the US Fish and Wildlife Service and Point Reyes Bird Observatory (Point Blue Conservation Science), biologist Scot Anderson created the Farallon Islands White Shark Project. Protection for white sharks soon followed. In January 1994, Title 14, California Code of Regulations, Fish and Game states that white sharks may not be taken. Federal regulations prohibit attracting white sharks with food, bait, chum, decoys, acoustics, or other means, or approaching them within 50 meters. (Courtesy Scot Anderson.)

GULLS SIGNALING SHARK FEEDING ACTIVITY, 1988. Waters off the Farallones are a hot spot for great white sharks due to the dense populations of marine mammals, the sharks' favored food group. When the Marine Mammal Act of 1972 ended the taking of seals, biologists noticed an increase in Red Triangle shark populations, due to the increased numbers of marine mammals in the area. Great white sharks have been protected in California waters since 1994. (Photograph by Scot Anderson.)

"Shark Man" Ron Elliott, Diving at Southeast Farallon Island. A respected commercial urchin diver from 1978 to 2004, Ron Elliott spent much of his career diving in the shark-populated waters off the Farallon Islands. After 2004, Elliott continued his diving career as an underwater photographer. He has had over 400 encounters with great white sharks at the Farallones: "The quietness—if a shark swims by, you don't hear it. There's no sound. It's silent." (Courtesy Ron Elliott.)

US Coast Guard Medevacs Diver Ron Elliott. On October 23, 2018, Elliott, who worked alone diving at the Farallones during his urchin-diving career, was medevaced off the research vessel *NorCal 1* by the US Coast Guard after suffering a shark bite on his right wrist and arm. He survived. Elliott is featured in the film *Near Miss*, about his encounter with a great white shark off the Farallones. (Courtesy Ron Elliott.)

JOSEPH LOCKE AND THE IMPOSSIBLE SWIM. On July 12, 2014, Joe Locke became the fourth person to swim from the Farallones to the Golden Gate. Marathon swimming from the shark-infested waters surrounding the Farallon Islands to the Golden Gate or adjacent mainland is an understandably unpopular sport that dates back to the 1967 swim by Stewart Evans (1926–1977), followed later that year by Ted Erickson, and in 2014 by Craig Lenning. In half a century, only four men and one woman have accomplished the seemingly impossible. (Courtesy Joe Locke.)

MARATHON SWIMMER KIMBERLY CHAMBERS, 2015. August 7–8, 2015, New Zealand–born Kimberly Chambers became the first woman and fifth person to swim from the Farallones to the Golden Gate. Hindered by high-running seas and seasickness, Chambers completed the swim in 17 hours, 12 minutes. As one open-water swimmer noted, these waters are "the coldest, windiest, bleakest, nastiest spot in the American Pacific." (Photograph by David McGuire.)

ROAD TO NOWHERE, 2016. A cement path that seemingly leads to the saddle in Seal Rock once led to a Radio Compass House built during World War II. The tower structure provided a transmitted signal for ships to use their radio direction finder (RDF) to get their bearings from the island. With the eventual demolition of the Radio Compass House, the remaining path serves as a road to nowhere. (Photograph by Ross Nichols; Point Blue.)

BURGEE OF THE ALL EIGHT CLUB, ESTABLISHED IN 1994. The flag's eight white stars, set in two groups, represent the four Northern and four Southern California Channel Islands. The All Eight Club was established in 1994 by the Santa Cruz Island Foundation to identify and honor those persons who have visited all eight California Channel Islands. To qualify, one must have walked on San Miguel, Santa Rosa, Santa Cruz, Anacapa, Santa Barbara, Santa Catalina, San Nicolas, and San Clemente Islands. Access to San Nicolas and San Clemente Islands is difficult due to their active military status. Members of the All Eight Club include biologists, anthropologists, botanists, ornithologists, zoologists, educators, helicopter and fixed-wing pilots, a retired National Park Service superintendent and park employees, a museum director, a lichenologist, a photographer, a retired judge, a sea captain, and a rock star. This is said to be the most exclusive recognized geographic club in the world, with membership in the low 200s—a quarter of the famous Seven Summits Club. (SCIF.)

Visit us at
arcadiapublishing.com

www.ingramcontent.com/pod-product-compliance
Lightning Source LLC
Chambersburg PA
CBHW060937170426
43194CB00027B/2981